RUNNING
Without
PAIN

A Guide to the
Prevention and Treatment
of Running Injuries

by Raymond Bridge

Illustrated by John Lencicki

THE DIAL PRESS · *New York* ·

This book is dedicated to
Ron and Tommie Farina and to
Dan and Jane Bowers—
good friends, running companions, and guinea pigs.

Published by
The Dial Press
1 Dag Hammarskjold Plaza
New York, New York 10017

Manufactured in the United States of America

FIRST PRINTING

Design by Dennis J. Grastorf

Library of Congress Cataloging in Publication Data

Bridge, Raymond.
  Running without pain.

  Includes index.
  1. Running—Accidents and injuries. 2. Sports
medicine. 3. Pain. I. Title.
RC1220.R8B74   617'.1027   79-17170
ISBN 0-8037-7395-3

Contents

INTRODUCTION: Runners and injuries. The   xi
frustrations and irony of running ailments.
The difficulties of finding medical care. The
ease with which most running injuries can be
completely prevented or arrested at an early
stage. Healing yourself and finding medical
help. The purpose of this book.

PART I: *THE BACKGROUND*

CHAPTER 1: FITNESS, CONDITIONING,
AND SAFETY   3
Beginners' pains and problems. The diseases
of a sedentary life. Cautions for neophytes.

Stress electrocardiograms. Building up. Conditioning pains and other complaints.

CHAPTER 2: GENERAL RULES FOR
PREVENTING INJURIES   12
Stress, adaptation, and breakdown. The dangers of being in good shape. Starting levels and safe rates of increase. Hard-easy patterns. Signs of overtraining. Peaking and recuperation. Weight. Coming back after a layoff. Stretching and supplementary exercises.

CHAPTER 3: MINOR IRRITATIONS AND
MALADIES   28
Chafing problems. Blisters: prevention and treatment. Calluses, corns, and warts. Toenail problems. Athlete's foot. Stitches. Shoulder and upper back pains. Numbness in the hands, arms, and legs.

CHAPTER 4: TYPES OF INJURIES   43
General types of injuries. Overuse injuries and their causes. Distinguishing between different types of injuries. Overtraining vs. structural problems. Strains and sprains. Tendon damage. Injuries to the bones. Bursitis. Heel bumps and spurs. Knee injuries. Other foot problems.

CHAPTER 5: TRAINING WITHOUT
INJURIES   64
How experienced runners should plan their training to avoid injuries. Shoes. Shoe maintenance.

CHAPTER 6: EVALUATING INJURIES
AND PAIN   77
   General principles of treatment. Muscle
   pulls. Tendon strains. Back pains. Hip pain.
   Thigh and groin injuries. Knee pain. Lower
   leg. Heel. Ankle. Bottom of foot. Forefoot.

CHAPTER 7: FINDING MEDICAL HELP   108
   Trainers, general practitioners, orthopedists,
   and podiatrists.

PART II: *STRETCHES AND EXERCISES*

CHAPTER 8: STRETCHING
FUNDAMENTALS   117
   Calisthenics and slow stretching. Stretching
   technique.   Stretching   opposing   muscle
   groups.

CHAPTER 9: BASIC STRETCHING
ROUTINES   124
   Making stretching a habit. Stretching the
   Achilles tendons. Stretching the lower area of
   the hamstrings. Stretching the upper ham-
   string area and the hip. Quadriceps, shins,
   and ankles: stretches for the front of the leg.
   Stretching the back.

CHAPTER 10: SPECIAL STRETCHES AND
MORE ADVANCED ROUTINES   132
   More stretches for the back. Stretching the
   front of the leg. Stretching the groin. A
   stretching sequence for the back and back of
   the legs. Stretches for the arms and shoulders.

CHAPTER 11: SPECIAL EXERCISES FOR
RUNNERS   138
    The disadvantages of running for physical
    conditioning. Preventing muscular imbal-
    ances. Special exercises to correct problems.
    Stretches that should be part of the runner's
    regular routine. Abdominal exercises. Exer-
    cises for the front of the legs.

CHAPTER 12: STAYING IN SHAPE
DURING A LAYOFF   142
    Psychological aspects of stopping running.
    Maintaining cardiovascular fitness. Planning
    a program. Bicycling. Swimming. Cross-
    country skiing. Rowing and paddling. Walk-
    ing. Weight training and calisthenics. Work-
    ing back into running without getting hurt.

PART III: ACCIDENTS, HEAT, AND COLD

CHAPTER 13: AVOIDING ACCIDENTAL
INJURIES   157
    Dangers to runners. Dealing with traffic.
    Making yourself visible. Defensive running.
    Footing and shoe stability. Dogs. Rabies and
    infection. Protecting your eyes. Running on
    ice.

CHAPTER 14: SPRAINS, BREAKS, AND
WOUNDS   170
    Dealing with traumatic injuries. Sprains.
    When to see a doctor. Getting over a sprain.
    Taping.

CHAPTER 15: COLD-WEATHER INJURIES 178
Running in cold weather. Flu and other respiratory infections. Hypothermia: prevention
and treatment. Frostbite and frostnip. Special
cautions for men. Breathing cold air. Bursitis.

CHAPTER 16: HEAT INJURIES 190
The dangers of hot weather. How the body
deals with heat. Heat acclimatization. Clothing. Fluids. Heat stroke. Heat exhaustion.
Cramps and dehydration.

PART IV: *INJURIES THAT BEGIN WITH
THE FEET*

CHAPTER 17: THE RUNNING BODY 203
How the runner moves. The legs and their
action. The knee and how it works.

CHAPTER 18: STRUCTURAL PROBLEMS
OF THE FEET 216
The motions of the foot. Pronation and su-
pination. The "normal" foot. Abnormal feet.
Analyzing your gait. Foot support. Taping
feet.

ADDITIONAL READING 236
INDEX 238

Introduction

I T's IRONIC that while regular runners are certainly the fittest large group in the United States, they're also among the most injury prone. Listen to any conversation in a group of runners and the most likely topic is injury. At the start of any race at least half the starters will bemoan the training time lost to tendonitis, pulled muscles, sore knees, heel spurs, and a host of other ailments. Even discounting the gamesmanship involved in these wailings, the number of running (or limping) wounded is amazing.

The purpose of this book is to help runners to avoid injuries and to deal with those they already have. Some injuries are probably inevitable for the serious, long-term runner, but I am convinced that the great majority can either be completely avoided or be successfully treated at an early stage, before they really become serious. The advantages of careful attention to the prevention of injuries should be obvious. Running is far more enjoyable when the body is free of pain and the mind is free of constant worry over the risk of worsening the damage that has already occurred. The erratic race performances and interruptions in training that result from injury can be eliminated, improving both the consistency and the quality of a racer's performances. Fitness runners and recreational runners can avoid the disruption of their routines and the setbacks to personal progress that always follow an injury.

Most important is the rediscovery of the joy of running. The sublime experiences of a unity of the body and spirit rarely occur when there are nagging pains in your legs and a constant worry about the level of training you can safely maintain. They certainly don't come when you are hobbling around in the grip of a serious running injury, wondering whether you'll ever be able to run again.

Runners and Injury

A dispassionate observer might well conclude that running is a pathological condition. Most of us who have established the running habit are true zealots. We bore our spouses, our nonrunning friends, and random victims at parties with paeans to running. We tout its benefits to physical conditioning, life expectancy, the joy of living, psychological health, and on and on ad nauseam. Yet a great many runners wage intermittent or constant battles with running-induced ailments. And the problem is not a passing one. The new crowds of converts to running are composed in large measure of older people and those who are not naturally talented. On an average, these runners are more susceptible to injury than younger runners and those who are physically well suited to the sport.

It is small wonder that doctors who are ignorant about running often warn their patients away from jogging and running with dire predictions of joint and tendon damage, if not heart attacks and strokes. Nor is it surprising that a lot of people thinking of taking up running or still experimenting with a little jogging are uncertain about the relative advantages and dangers of the sport for middle-aged nonathletes.

For addicted runners injuries have often been a source of trial and frustration. Many ailments strike just when the athlete feels at his peak, devastating the hopes of the serious competitor and setting the recreational runner back for months. Even worse has been the difficulty of understanding the nature and causes of many problems and the general lack of interest from the medical profession.

Until very recently most doctors showed little sympathy or understanding for the problems of injured athletes. This was particularly true for the mature amateur engaged in athletics for its own sake. The usual response to the runner trying to find a cure for some ailment in the feet, legs, or lower back was "Act your age and stop trying to compete with the kids!" Alternatively, a doctor would impatiently instruct the runner to lay off until the problem went away, with the clear implication that the sort of pain arising from running was not worth serious attention in a practice that concerned itself with people who were *really* sick.

Of course there is a certain validity to the feeling that the medical problems of the runner are not in the same league as those of the cancer victim or heart patient. A doctor might feel that ministering to the aches and pains of the distance runner is a bit of a comedown from the life-and-death work of the more dramatic areas of medicine. It is equally true, though, that an expensive heart surgeon could save far more lives by operating a clinic in India or Appalachia. But few of us would conclude that the successful operations he performs are not worthwhile.

The most interesting side of sports medicine, especially that concerned with running injuries, is that it is a medicine of health. The regular runner greatly reduces the chance of contracting cardiovascular disease and a host of other degenerative diseases. Rather than destroying his health with cigarettes, overeating, or sedentary living, the runner maintains a far better level of general health than does the bulk of the population. The minor ailments associated with running can be viewed as side effects of a generally healthy life-style, and are certainly preferable to lung cancer, emphysema, and heart disease. It may well be that the podiatrist who helps to heal runners' feet and legs saves more lives than the glamorous surgeon.

For the runner suffering through an injury, however, there is never any question about the importance of the pain and disability. For many of us, running is a major part of our lives, and an injury that interferes with it is as distressing as any other major disruption at work, at school, or in our family life. In the strain to run through the injury, keep up other forms of training, or heal the damage and start running again, we often become obsessive. Some of us have more problems of this sort than others; but, for a while at least, the inability to run takes on far more importance than the running when we're able to do it. We tend to take running—like many other features of our lives—for granted; and when we are unable to run, the loss is felt more keenly.

All this is easy enough to deal with when the cause of the problem is well understood and the end in sight. Thus when a bout of flu stops you from running in winter, it's just one of those minor adversities that are part of any endeavor. But there is a special frustration associated with nagging injuries that can't be pinned down, particularly when doctors shrug their shoulders or try to bluff their way through an ailment they obviously don't understand. Runners in this situation will often try any remedy, from bee pollen to new shoes, ultrasound to orthotics.

Fortunately, with the explosion in running, experience with various kinds of injuries and training programs has grown immensely, and our understanding of the causes of many injuries and the means to prevent them has grown. If the runner listens to his body, training can be tailored to produce good results without causing injury, and the problems that do occur can usually be handled effectively before they become too serious.

The tremendous increase in the popularity of running has also helped to push the medical profession into reexamining its attitudes about the treatment of sports injuries. Podiatry, the branch of medicine specializing in the foot, has discovered the similarities between patients who have traditionally needed special care and runners, and the podiatrist is rapidly replacing the coach as the most important counselor to aspiring Olympians. There are now also quite a few physicians who are runners themselves, so it is usually possible for the runner with major problems to find a sympathetic ear and some knowledge of the runner's medical problems.

The growth in interest in running injuries and the increased knowledge about them are exciting developments, full of potential; but in any field as new as this one there is as much opinion floating around as firm knowledge. Information can be hard to come by. The more the runner knows, however, the better equipped he will be to prevent injuries from occurring, treat them successfully if they do occur, find good medical help when necessary, assist the doctor in diagnosis, and judge the quality of the medical care received.

Healing Yourself

The purpose of this book is to help you to prevent and heal your own running injuries, with a doctor's help if necessary. The most important rule of maintaining health is to take care of your own body. One of the insidious aspects of disease-oriented medicine is our tendency to view doctors as technicians, like auto or TV repairmen. When something goes wrong with the machine, you take it to the specialist to get it fixed. ("Could you have it ready for the marathon next weekend?") This view is false, of course. The body will heal itself if you give it a chance, and the doctor may be able to help you understand what's wrong and facilitate the healing process. But if you abuse your body, no amount of sophisticated medical paraphernalia will save you from the consequences.

Most running injuries are the result of bad training. Runners typically recognize the dangers of overstress for others, but they fail to apply the same rules to themselves. They can easily see the cause of someone else's tendonitis in a too-fast buildup for a marathon, but even the most mild-mannered runners somehow think of themselves as supermen or superwomen when they are training hard. Much of this book is therefore concerned with avoiding this type of injury. Only you can maintain the fine balance between stressing your body in a healthy way and pushing it past its ability to adapt.

Mechanical problems in the feet, legs, and back often contribute to overstress injuries. After all, the weakest links will give way first. Remember, though, that shoe modifications and special supports merely even out the stresses in the body. They are not magic talismans that make you immune to injury. Many people will be helped to run painlessly with these devices, but they can still hurt themselves by overtraining, inadequate stretching, and the like.

For all these reasons I consider the earlier parts of this book to be the most important and basic. They cover the principles of avoiding injuries through the proper balance of training, stretching, and supplementary exercises. The mechanical problems discussed later in the book are fairly common, but they are less important than good training technique in avoiding injuries. In fact, those who have mechanical problems with their feet and legs have to plan their training far more carefully than do runners with perfect feet. All the causes of injury are additive. That is why it is generally useless to search for single explanations and for magic solutions. For every injury that will respond dramatically to a new shoe or arch support or orthotic, there are a dozen that require a combination of approaches for successful treatment. To heal yourself you have to think through your problems carefully and patiently, with the assistance of a doctor if necessary. Grasping impatiently for the latest syndrome or shoe or podiatrist and then switching a few days later will not get you through.

Self-Treatment and Medical Treatment

This book is not intended as a substitute for competent medical help. For those with joint damage in the knee, for example, there is no substitute for evaluation by a good orthopedic specialist, and the years of training in the mechanics of the foot received by the podiatrist cannot be replaced by a layman's introduction like this one. I am not a doctor, and this book is not a medical text. Furthermore, the dangers of being one's own specialist are recognized in every profession, from law to medicine, even for those who have elaborate training. It is difficult to weed out your emotions and desires so that you can develop an analytical approach to your problem.

For both of these reasons it is important to seek out medical help when you seem to need it. The techniques available to the podiatrist or orthopedist for analyzing gait and injuries cannot be duplicated by any sort of self-analysis, and all running injuries can develop additional complications if they are allowed to continue without treatment.

On the other hand, most of the problems of runners are not particularly difficult to understand, and poor diagnoses in the past have amply demonstrated that the qualifications of running experience are as necessary as medical experience. I firmly believe also that the runner who has a good grasp of the nature and causes of running injuries will be much better able to get successful treatment from a physician than a runner who is ill informed.

Finally, though the doctor has a battery of techniques available, from gait analysis and X rays to arthrograms, the runner himself has probably the most sensitive analytical tool of all: the feeling of his body during each of the thousands of steps that occur on a training run. If you learn the rudiments of running mechanics and the art of listening to your body, you can often catch difficulties in an incipient stage and effect a cure long before a visit to a doctor's office is necessary. I hope that this book will help more runners to enjoy their sport without the long bouts of pain and injury that spoil the joys of running.

Part I

THE
BACKGROUND

CHAPTER 1

Fitness, Conditioning, and Safety

THIS CHAPTER is concerned primarily with injuries and hazards peculiar to beginning runners and joggers—those who cover distances in the range of a mile or two a day. The pains and problems of the newcomer to running are really quite different from those that are likely to plague the experienced runner, something the veteran is likely to forget when counseling the novice. Nor are the appropriate training techniques the same. It is important for the new enthusiast to bear this in mind when starting to read publications written for runners. The neophyte is likely to come across programs for speed and interval training that are completely inappropriate for someone at his stage of development.

In evaluating opinions about both injuries and training

methods, it is important to determine whom the author is really addressing, consciously or not. Keep in mind that most people writing articles and books for runners have been at the sport for a long time and may well have forgotten what it was like to start. More important still, a lot of them have been running at least since their high school years and have never had the experience of starting running at the age of thirty-five or forty-five.

This is evident from some of the training programs that have been published, particularly for marathons. Many such prescriptions are based on an unrealistic notion of the time required to move from the conditioning level of the average American adult to that of a serious runner. Unfortunately, a lot of people thus have expectations that are completely unrealistic when they start running. This is a prescription for injury, and in the case of beginners the injury may be very serious indeed.

The position of the rank beginner is paradoxical. The novice is less likely to develop serious mechanical damage in the legs and feet than the runner with highly trained lungs and heart. The average American adult is in such poor overall shape that he finds it impossible to run very long or very fast—an odd sort of protection from the kinds of overuse injuries normally experienced by the serious runner. By and large, the average beginner will run out of breath or stamina before developing Achilles tendonitis. The neophyte will get sore muscles, but rarely serious muscle pulls. Unfortunately, he may also have a heart attack, which would be highly unusual in the runner who is regularly putting in ten miles a day.

The Dangers of the Sedentary Life

The contradictory state of health of most Americans is particularly striking to anyone familiar with conditions in poorer countries. On the one hand, many of the horrible communicable diseases and parasitic infestations that plague nearly half the people in the world have been wiped out so thoroughly here that they are virtually unknown. Our public health and sanitation systems are sufficiently well developed that a minor outbreak of one of the major diseases that have decimated societies through the ages is likely to be an occasion for an inquiry into the negligence of local health authorities. Most of the grosser deficiency diseases are also fairly rare, or at least hidden in pockets of society out of view of the great majority. If one ignores the wholesale spreading of poorly understood organic contaminants into the environment and the dangers of radioactive wastes, we might seem in a superficial view to have reached the millennium in the area of public health.

On the other hand, the average inhabitant of one of the "underdeveloped" countries, goiter and all, could easily walk most Americans into the ground. In Nepal, villagers hired as porters, including women and children, regularly carry for weeks on end over steep mountain trails loads that few Americans could haul for a block. Quite a few carry double loads of 120 pounds or so for distances that a lot of our people would have difficulty walking with no baggage at all. As a people we are overfed and underexercised. Our bodies have atrophied from lack of use and are plugged with the debris of too much rich food.

And we pay the price. The incidence of cardiovascular disease and other disorders associated with our sedentary lifestyle is enormous, far greater than in the underdeveloped world. Regular exercise will reverse most of this deterioration after a while, but the beginning runner first has to worry about the effects that years of disuse may already have caused. The diseases of the heart and blood vessels, together with weakened muscles and lack of flexibility, may flare up to confront the neophyte trying to make up for years of inactivity.

At least as early as adolescence, young people in the United States begin to build up the deposits in their arteries that ultimately result in diseases of the blood vessels and the heart, at least in the more susceptible individuals. A person who already has a well-developed case of heart disease, whether or not it has been detected, is quite likely to precipitate a heart attack by going out and running to near exhaustion. This does not mean that running *causes* heart disease; quite the contrary. If the individual didn't bring on the attack by running, something else would serve the same purpose a little later on. In fact, a carefully graded running program is one of the best preventives against heart attack and an excellent method of reversing the progress of cardiovascular disease. The slow progression of such a program is critical, however, and if there is any reason to suspect cardiovascular disease, a running program should be started only in consultation with a physician.

Those who are statistically the most vulnerable are men past their mid-thirties. Women ten to fifteen years older are in the same position, and with recent social changes the age differential is diminishing. Other predisposing factors should also be considered, including excess weight, smoking, high blood pressure, and a history of family heart disease. Most of these are well-known and will not be discussed in detail here. Readers interested in a detailed system of evaluating their fitness for running and in a graded program to match can find a point system in my *Runner's Book*. Specific recommendations can also be found in Kenneth Cooper's *New Aerobics*.

The readers of this book, most of whom have already run

for a while, at least can feel much more comfortable. With each level of cardiovascular conditioning, the probability of heart attack is certainly reduced, though claims of complete immunity at any level are probably overstated.

Those still at the beginner's level, however, should remain cautious about increasing their levels of stress too rapidly. If you have been jogging a mile or two three times a week, you have already demonstrated that you aren't in the highest risk category, but if you are middle-aged or beyond, it would be prudent to increase your distance and speed cautiously. The most common form of heart attack is caused by a failure of circulation within the heart itself. The heart muscle is starved of oxygen and nutrients, and the cells die. If some vessels are partially closed off, endurance exercises will stimulate the heart to bypass them by developing other vessels to greater capacity. All this takes time, however, and placing high demands on the heart too rapidly can result in damage.

If you have any worries about your running, or if you have a number of risk factors, it may be worthwhile to have a physical examination and a stress electrocardiogram, which can reveal many circulatory problems before they are noticed. If you have had any pains in the chest, arms, shoulders, or back that seem to be related to intensity of exercise, don't do any more running until you've had a thorough checkup. That is, if the pains appear when you are running, when you reach a hill, or after you speed up, they are directly related to the demands being made on your heart. Such signs are often felt in other parts of the upper body rather than in the chest near the heart. This kind of warning should *never* be ignored.

The stress electrocardiogram is like the normal ECG—a recording of the electrical activity of the heart—except that it is taken during exercise, so that it records what your heart does when it is working hard. Many irregularities show up on a stress test that would not be apparent on an ECG taken at rest. Most doctors recommend a stress ECG for anyone over thirty or thirty-five years old before beginning a running program. If you are already running or jogging regularly, a little common sense should tell you whether you need a test. If you are worried, it's certainly worth having one. It makes sense to go to a doctor familiar with running, however. The ideal is to go to one of the centers that specialize in testing people who are starting exercise programs. Such centers typically give a whole battery of tests, including a stress ECG, fat content and blood composition tests, finally giving you a specific program for improving your condition, including target heart rates to achieve in exercising.

My own approach tends more toward anarchy and less toward the mechanistic, but there is no doubt that such centers greatly reduce the guesswork both about your health at the start of an exercise program and about the best plan for improvement.

The most important prescription for avoiding a heart attack during your initial period of recovery from a sedentary lifestyle, however, is the same as the one for avoiding most other injuries that beginning runners experience: *Take it easy!* Most of us have a tendency to take an all-or-nothing approach. We want our resolution that we will change our ways to produce immediate rewards. To achieve immediate results we are willing to work extra hard. The type of person who takes up running seems to be particularly compulsive this way. This is a theme that will crop up again and again in this book, because it is a problem one can observe in runners ranging from the brand-new jogger, huffing and puffing up the block in his new warm-up suit, to the Olympic contender trying to push from one peak period to another without a recovery in between. It is a guaranteed recipe for trouble.

Building Up

The cardinal rule for all runners, from beginners to serious competitors, is *Stress the body at gradually increasing levels of exertion.* Stress is one of the fundamental ingredients of life. It is a good thing. Your body will adapt to physical stresses and become stronger as a result, but only if it is stressed within its limits. By making your body work harder than usual, you will stimulate it to strengthen itself so that it can deal with the same levels of difficulty in the future. If you stress yourself too much, however, you'll exceed your body's adaptive ability, and it will break down.

One of the important skills for the serious runner is learning to gauge both the stress applied and the body's adaptive capacity so accurately as to be able to achieve maximum performance. This is a very delicate balance, and a small error in judgment can precipitate a breakdown, whether in the form of a foot or leg injury or as a cold, the flu, or mononucleosis. This fine tuning will be discussed in more detail in later chapters. For the beginner the important lesson is to stay well clear of the borderline area where the body's adaptive capacity is strained.

The beginner has to learn to be concerned with progress that is slow but steady rather than rapid and erratic. Trying to push too hard will lead to illness and injury, which set progress back much farther than the distance that might have been lost by progressing a little more moderately to begin with.

Thus for the true beginner a running program may actually start with vigorous walks, alternate walking and jogging, or easy jogging for periods of thirty minutes to an hour. Faster intervals are gradually introduced and the overall pace picked up through the months. The emphasis should always be on longer sessions at easy to moderate levels of stress, however, rather than on short and exhausting bursts of speed.

Conditioning Pains

The most common difficulties experienced by the beginner come from stiff and aching muscles. Such aches and pains are an indication of doing a little too much at a time, but they should not cause any real concern. Tissue is broken down and waste products built up in the process of training, and the usual beginner's aches and pains are a result of this process. Continued regular exercise will eliminate these feelings, which are also common among well-conditioned athletes who resume training after a layoff, even a brief one. Like the novice, they try to start at a higher level of exertion than their bodies are currently conditioned for.

Warm-up and cool-down periods accompanied by stretching before and after running will reduce these aches and stiffness. These techniques are discussed in detail in later chapters. But there are several important warnings the beginner should observe to prevent more serious problems from developing.

The most important of these admonitions is *Don't try to push yourself into good condition by sheer willpower*. If you try to run a little faster and farther every day, especially when your legs are sore from previous efforts, you will develop real injuries, far graver than mere soreness of the muscles. There is simply no substitute for regular exercise and slow increases in intensity. Real progress in overall conditioning is sure but fairly slow. Forcing a peak by pushing hard will result in predictable declines in performance soon after, often accompanied by injury.

Make a distinction between stiffness or soreness in the leg muscles and sore joints, sharp muscular pains, and aches in the tendons—particularly the Achilles tendons, extending from the heels to the base of the calf muscles. All these latter symptoms may be warnings of impending injuries, and they should be a signal to slow down and reduce stress until they have cleared. Later chapters in the book discuss such problems in more detail.

Another important warning sign is a general lackluster feeling, a sign of overstress. More detailed discussion of the signs of overtraining can be found on pages 20–22. Learning to recognize and heed such warnings is among the most valuable things a runner can learn. They are just as important to the serious competitive runner as to the neophyte, and you will need to watch for them throughout your running career.

Other Complaints

Various forms of chafing and abrasion are particularly annoying to the beginning runner. Most runners build up a resistance to these maladies as they go on, except on unusual occasions. Chafing on the insides of the thighs is common, particularly if you are a little overweight. Make sure that your shorts or the seams of your running pants are smooth there. Even a small rough edge can become a major irritant over the miles. Liberal applications of petroleum jelly are the best remedy when your thighs are rubbing against each other.

The same solution is helpful for chafing under the armpits, on the nipples, and around the edges of bras. The latter two spots may need applications of adhesive tape, Band-Aids, or moleskin if Vaseline doesn't work. Women who have troubles with bras may need to search out a brand that has no irritating hardware or stiff fabric. Problems of abrasion on the feet are discussed in detail in Chapter Three. Though they are mainly a problem for beginners, some people with sensitive feet have to take special care no matter how long they run.

CHAPTER 2

General Rules for
Preventing Injuries

RUNNERS are an odd lot. Many are outwardly rather mild mannered, yet the drive that is apparent in their training belies their seemingly easygoing demeanor. The compulsive striving of many runners is probably the single most important cause of injuries. Furthermore, runners are as bad as smokers in their apparently firm belief that "it can't happen to me!" No one ever says that, of course, but deep down inside they believe it.

Most experienced runners these days know that overtraining can be dangerous—for someone else. But they don't apply the understanding to themselves. There seems to be the feeling that if one just tries a little harder and works a little more, the results will be proportionate. This dangerous attitude is particularly prevalent among those who have been running for a couple of years and are thrilled at the difference in their physical condition. They decide to run a marathon or to complete one in a better time, and they increase their training in large bounds. Women can be as compulsive in this respect as men, with equally disastrous consequences.

Stress, Adaptation, and Breakdown

The basic principles that the runner needs to understand to prevent injury are the same ones that are fundamental to good training. The foundation of any training program is the ability of the body to adapt to repeated stress. Muscles function most efficiently at much less than their ultimate capacity, and they respond to the normal work load placed on them by developing the capacity to function reasonably well at the level of work they are normally called on to perform. If the normal work load consists of walking back and forth to the coffee machine a couple of times a day, and to the refrigerator on evenings and weekends, the muscles will gradually atrophy until they are able to perform efficiently at just that level of work.

On the other hand, if the muscles are used regularly in fairly strenuous exercise, they will increase their strength and endurance to meet the demands placed on them. The ability to work harder thus flows from hard work. The muscles adapt themselves to regular stress or to the lack of it. There are a number of subtleties that qualify this principle in important ways, however.

To begin with, adaptation is quite specific. Though there are certain carryovers from one activity to another, they are limited. Doing exercises that increase the strength or endurance of the legs will have no significant effect on the arms. Furthermore, stressing a muscle to increase its absolute strength for a short period of time will have little influence on the endurance capacity of the muscle. Developing the ability to lift a heavy weight will not help you to run a marathon. Even practice in the 100-meter dash will not be very useful to the marathoner, except perhaps as a supplement to more specific training.

The specificity of training has many applications for the regular runner, though there are precautions that must be associated with it also. The most important consequence is that to run long-distance, the distance runner must train with basically the same activity. The primary requirements for this kind of running are cardiovascular fitness and *sufficient strength in the structure of the lower body to withstand the stresses involved*. We will deal with particular methods of training later, but it is important to understand that the body will adapt to this type of stress only by being subjected to similar work regularly and frequently.

The second major principle of stress and adaptation is that the levels involved are critical. The body adapts only when it is stimulated. If you apply too little stress, there is no stimulus for the body to improve its conditioning. It will slide backward if the stimulus is low enough or infrequent enough. Too much stress, however, will result in destruction rather than adaptation.

There is a fine line here, and following it is the crucial test of those who are attempting to achieve maximum conditioning. Some tissue is broken down in good training, and the body replaces it with new tissue better adapted to perform under the stress encountered. But too much stress causes injury, and the body then requires a long period of healing. Attempts to stress it even more in an injured condition may result in a total breakdown.

Both the level of stress and its frequency are important elements in determining whether the body will adapt or break down. Not only is it wrong to try to run too far, too fast; it is even worse to do so too often. The adaptation the runner is seeking from training takes time, and repeated stress is useful only when the body has had time to recover from the last workout. Individuals are different, and adaptation time can be improved, but experienced runners are far more likely to run too many hard workouts than too few. It is always better to err on the low side when you are training seriously.

The consequences of undertraining are really quite trivial, particularly for those of us who are not trying for the 1980 Olympic team. We may run a little slower in a race, peak a little later than we had planned, or reach a particular level of conditioning a month or two later than we hoped. Overtraining is likely to disable the runner for months. Instead of running the race a little slower, you may not finish at all, and your conditioning is set back for a long period instead of merely progressing a little more slowly.

This is particularly true for those of us past thirty. Our healing and adaptive powers are weaker than they were at the age of twenty. One of the pleasures of distance running is that one's performance level is not radically altered by middle age. It is a little lower, but potential isn't nearly as important as the effects of training. Thus the forty-five- or sixty-five-year-old marathoner can pass crowds of people in their twenties who are not as well trained. One thing that is affected, though, is your resilience. You can't adapt to stress as quickly, so you have to make up the difference with staying power. A major cause of injuries is that a lot of middle-aged runners are trying to follow training schedules devised by people used to working with college track teams. Instead of improving, many of them break down.

The Danger of Being in Good Shape

The regular runner who is trying to improve his general

condition or to prepare for some special event like a marathon needs to pay particular attention to one aspect of training. At the beginner's level the limiting factor in performance is usually cardiopulmonary condition. For the more experienced runner, this is not normally the case. You can improve your cardiopulmonary performance faster than the ability of your body to tolerate the mechanical stresses involved. You can double your training mileage or up your speed enormously overnight—for a little while. Your lungs and heart won't give out, but there is a good chance that your knees, your hamstrings, or your Achilles tendons will.

The ability of the musculoskeletal system to adapt is slower than that of the lungs and cardiovascular system, and this is particularly true of bones and joints. Bones do thicken and become stronger when the additional strength is needed. Joints often strengthen, too; but the process is slow, and the results of overwork can be very unpleasant. Furthermore, the process of adaptation and injury in some of these areas is very poorly understood. For example, if you have had past injuries to your knees and have some difficulty with them, no doctor will be able to tell you whether running of gradually increasing intensity will ultimately cause your knees to get better or deteriorate. One thing is certain: If you try to increase your running speed and distance too fast, your knees will break down.

Running is one of the most powerful tools for conditioning the body. You can control the amount of cardiovascular stress you impose on your body as you can in very few activities. Running is particularly attractive to those who are busy with other activities, because they can accomplish more with a limited and flexible investment of time than they could with almost any other form of exercise. Like many another powerful tool, however, running can be dangerous if it is not used intelligently. Because you can exercise such enormous control over the amount that you stress yourself, you have to be careful not to do too much. The more you drive yourself, the more careful you have to be. Use your willpower to stick with your training schedule or to call up reserves in races, not to push yourself beyond your body's capacity in training.

Starting Levels and Safe Increases

When talking about increases in levels of training, it is always difficult to be specific, because people begin at such widely varying levels. For the beginner a fast pace may be ten or twelve minutes a mile, while for a well-trained runner who is reasonably quick, seven-minute miles may be moderate jogging. Similarly, for the neophyte, a workout that involves continuous jogging for a couple of miles may be so far out of reach that it seems impossible, while many serious distance runners do twenty-five- or thirty-mile workouts at least once a week.

In considering safe training increases, you can approach the problem from a number of points of view, but you need to have some idea of your starting level first. Weekly averages make a fairly convenient basis of reference, whether you use mileage or time as a base, and whether you keep detailed records or merely work from a basic knowledge of what you do. By considering average weekly mileage, days off are averaged in and the overall effects of daily fluctuations are automatically considered. There is an enormous difference in the training level of two runners who both periodically run a maximum of ten miles in training if one of them averages seventy miles a week and the other thirty.

Your base level of training is essentially the one that you can handle comfortably *now*, on a regular basis, week in and week out. A single hundred-mile week does not mean that you are starting from a weekly base of a hundred miles if your usual weekly total is fifty. If you try to repeat the high mileage for two more weeks in a row, you'll probably start to break down.

I think that it is dangerous to try to increase training mileage at a rate of more than 10 percent each week. This is an average figure. You probably won't get hurt if you go up 20 percent and then stay there for two or three weeks, but if you try to jump 20 percent two or three weeks in a row, you stand a good chance of running into trouble. The same formula works just as well using time instead of mileage, providing the intensity is roughly the same.

Intensity is just as critical as mileage or time spent on the road. If you are increasing your speed, introducing hill workouts, or starting hard sessions on the track, you should not try to up your mileage at the same time. As with adding mileage too quickly, this sort of doubling is more likely to result in a serious injury than in improved performance.

These rates of increase are recommended only as a provisional *maximum*, not as a progression you should try to follow. The most important rule for gauging your progress is to follow the dictates of your own body. The 10-percent rule is useful when you are thinking about tentative plans. For example, if you are considering a twenty-mile race in two months and estimate that you need to run at least fifty miles a week for the month before, you should ask what sort of mileage you are running now. If you are currently doing 25 miles a week, your first 10 percent increase would bring you to 27.5, the next to 30.25, and so on. You would not even reach 50 miles a week until nearly the time of the race, and would not have time to level off and become used to the mileage. You should skip the race and give yourself more time to prepare, or plan to run it on lower training, recognizing that you will have to be satisfied with a slow pace.

The Hard/Easy Pattern

Besides controlling your overall attempts to increase stress, it is important not to try to work hard every day. The scientific basis for this rule is that recovery from a stressful workout requires more than a day for most people. Imposing additional stress on muscles that have not yet recuperated from the last session does not result in more rapid improvement, and it often causes injury if repeated too often. Your rate of recovery is an individual thing, and you may find that it changes with time. For most runners, however, a hard day/easy day schedule like the one devised by Oregon coach Bill Bowerman works well.

In its most general form, the idea is simply to run a good workout one day and to do one that does not extend your capacity the next. For example, a runner who is doing basic distance training covering around sixty to sixty-five miles a week might run ten miles at a good clip one day and jog a relaxed five or six the next, taking a single twenty-mile run on Saturday or Sunday. A competitive runner sharpening for a racing season might, over the period of a week, alternate three hard workouts on the track or two hard workouts and one time trial (a fast run at race pace) with easy distance runs on the days in between.

There is a myth still vaguely accepted by many runners that if one hard workout is good, two must be better. This nonsense is left over from the tough-guy, "running through the pain" era of coaching. It simply isn't so. Even world champions, who are capable of withstanding more hard workouts than the average runner, cannot usually tolerate this sort of training. Many of the legendary hard men who ran difficult workouts every day ultimately broke down under the strain. Very few runners have profited from constantly hard training routines, but a lot have been ruined by them. Quite a few runners, including some champions, have found that they need two easy days after every hard one. The point is to find out what works for you, without letting preconceptions cloud your judgment.

Signs of Overtraining

The single most important way of preventing injuries over the years is to learn to recognize the signs of overtraining in yourself and to heed them by reducing the work load on your body. The body usually gives clear warning signs before breaking down, provided that the runner is willing to pay attention. When we hurt ourselves badly, it is usually after we have ignored the symptoms of overuse for some time and pushed on toward some goal that is foremost in our minds.

Overtraining may manifest itself in some of the general signs mentioned below, or it may show up in the beginnings of a specific injury. Overuse injuries of various types will often be the first sign that you are training too hard. They typically occur when you have exceeded the capacity of your body to adapt to the increased workload. Thus your knees may start to hurt because of too heavy an increase in speed or distance, while they might be able to tolerate the extra stress if it were applied more gradually. Naturally, the weakest parts of the body give way first, so this type of injury is most likely to occur in places that often trouble you, even if the injury is due to overtraining and not to some other cause.

For these reasons the first cause you should suspect if you start to have pain in an Achilles tendon, a knee, or one of your quadriceps is that you have been training too hard. Think about your recent running and look through your training diary to see whether this could be the cause. Don't dismiss it because you've run at the same level before, or because you've built up at the same rate on other occasions. The body is different from one day and one month to the next. There are fluctuations in its ability to adapt, especially if other demands are added. If you are a little overweight, you impose additional stress on the body. If you are under strain at work or are not getting enough sleep, you won't be able to tolerate as much stress in your running. Keep in mind that you are quite capable of pushing yourself hard enough over a long period to drain your body's reserves completely and dangerously.

The following are some of the general signs of overstress:

1. Aching or sore legs. We're talking here not about specific injuries to a particular joint, muscle, or tendon, but simply of mild generalized pain or heaviness. This occurs when you have been working too hard, and you should stick to easy running until it disappears.

2. Changes in your usual habits and routines, such as: fatigue, excess sleep or insomnia, clumsiness, difficulty in concentrating, irritability, or a washed-out attitude.

3. Susceptibility to colds or flu. Some runners break out in acne or get cold sores when they become run down. If you begin to feel that you have no resilience left, it is important to let up. It is no coincidence that many runners go through a constant pattern of missing big races for which they are preparing because they come down with flu or a bad cold. Their resistance is lowered by overtraining.

4. A drop in weight accompanied by chronic thirst, or amber-colored urine, both signs of dehydration. These are to be expected after a long run in hot weather, but

should not persist from day to day. Chronic dehydration is dangerous.

5. A resting pulse that is higher than usual. This is a sign that your body has not recuperated from earlier stress. It is normal for several hours after a run, but not from one day to the next.

6. Poor performance persisting for several days. Don't try to "push through" your slump. It is a sign that you've drawn too much on your reserves and need to back off for a while. Forcing yourself to keep training harder will probably result in a serious breakdown.

Peaking and Recuperating

Some principles of training to achieve good performance without injury are discussed in more detail in Chapter Five, but the phenomenon of peaking is important even for the beginner. It explains the common and frustrating fluctuation between rapid progress and stagnation. Training does not proceed in a steady upward curve of constantly better performances, particularly for racers and other runners who often push themselves near their limits. Your performances will vary from time to time, and though the overall level may continue to improve from one year to the next, there will be intervening periods when your achievements will be disappointing.

You can think of this oscillation as being similar to the daily patterns of running fast sometimes and at a relaxed pace in other workouts. If you try to run as hard as you can all the time, your performance will never be very good, and you may well become so badly hurt or so physically depleted that you will stop running altogether. There are peak periods in performance, just as there are daily peaks and peaks within a particular run or race. And just as you can arrange to perform at your best level on a racing day (if you are a racer), you can also plan to come to an overall peak during a particular season. What you cannot do is maintain your peak all the time and build on it. If you try, you will decline in overall performance and probably hurt yourself in the bargain.

Serious racers should intentionally peak at the times when they want to turn in the best performances. The recent master of this art has been Lasse Viren, the great Finnish distance runner who won the Gold Medal in both the 5,000- and 10,000-meter events in the 1972 Olympics and then repeated the performance in 1976. After 1976 there was a lot of foolish gossip in athletic circles about "blood doping,"* because Viren had not performed particularly well in races prior to the Olympics. The real lesson the scandalmongers should have learned was that Viren was smart enough to peak for the races he wanted to win, instead of the less important competitions before and after. Though athletes are different in the variation between their peak and off-peak performances, most of them do follow this pattern, either intentionally or not. The intelligent ones learn to plan their peaks.

The noncompetitor needs to recognize this same pattern to avoid both disappointment and injury. If you have been

---

* Blood doping is the technique of giving an athlete a transfusion of his or her own blood just prior to an athletic event. The blood is removed several weeks before and kept under refrigeration. The idea is that during the intervening period the body will replace the lost blood, and that the added blood will then provide a larger number of red corpuscles and thus a greater oxygen-carrying capacity. It is highly questionable whether the technique will work if it is used, because the body may dispose of fluid components of the blood to reduce it to normal volume, and the remainder may be too thick to move through the blood vessels normally. Performance thus seems as likely to be worsened as improved.

working for a while doing distance on the roads, building up a good base of conditioning, you will find that a month of speed work will bring about vast improvements in your running during a relatively short time. You will probably be able to retain some of these gains, so that your basic speed will be greater than it was before. The spectacular improvement will not keep up, however. The degree to which performance falls off is usually closely related to the sharpness of the hard training that produced it. If you want the peak to last longer and fall off less sharply, it is usually best to work your speed up slowly, with fewer really hard interval and speed sessions. The serious runner should keep a careful record of training and performances, learning to control peaking to obtain the desired results.

For our purposes here the main point is to use the natural rhythms of your body rather than trying to fight them. If you've had wonderful improvements in the past six weeks, but you begin to feel stale and have to fight to repeat efforts that were easy and enjoyable a few weeks before, recognize that you are coming off a peak. Relax, and don't try to force your way through. Do most of your runs at a comfortable pace for a while, and forget about times for a little.

Weight

Body weight is an important element of the overall stress that a runner imposes on his system. Running ten miles in sixty minutes is a lot harder after you gain five pounds. When you are carrying extra weight, all the muscles involved in running have to do a little more work with every step. Your heart, circulatory system, and lungs have to supply the extra fatty tissue with oxygen and nutrients. Your bones, joints, tendons, muscles, and ligaments have to absorb extra stress each time one of your feet hits the pavement. Running is simply harder on your body when you are overweight.

All this is not mentioned as some kind of puritanical tract. There is no rule that says all runners have to be in perfect racing shape, carrying only a tiny percentage of body fat. It is important to recognize, however, that extra weight is literally a heavy burden on your whole body. The more excess weight you are carrying, the more you are stressing yourself by doing any particular mileage at a given speed.

A few extra pounds may easily tip the balance to the injury side if you are close to the limits of your joints and tendons. Remember that all of your muscular and skeletal structure is made of living tissue, constantly being renewed. Many running injuries occur when the regenerative capacity can't keep pace with the damage being done. Eventually something gives way. If an area under stress is barely being repaired as fast as it is being broken down, the addition of five or ten pounds to the weight pounding on it will throw the balance off.

For these reasons it is important to keep your weight in mind when you are responding to your desires and ambitions. It is a critical factor in your training plans. If you are not at a competitive weight, the best single thing you can do to improve performance is to get rid of the fat. My personal opinion is that no one who is much over racing weight should do any serious interval or speed work.

It doesn't make sense to go to a track and grind out ten miles of intervals when you are fifteen or twenty-five pounds over a decent racing weight. Either stay on base training or—if you want to do some serious racing—lose weight! Then start sharpening with intervals. You'll race faster and be a lot less likely to get hurt.

Coming Back After a Layoff

One of the most frustrating experiences for the regular runner is the first run after a long layoff. Conditioning proceeds in either direction, and your capacity declines rather quickly when you stop running. This is particularly true of the fine edge that develops when you are sharpening for a race. A couple of weeks off the roads and trails and you feel like a struggling beginner again. (It isn't really that bad, but it seems so.)

There is a tremendous temptation in this situation to try to start up where you left off: at the same mileages, the same speeds, and with the same expectations or even higher ones—making up for the time lost in a schedule, for example. *Don't do it!* If your training schedule was properly thought out in the first place, with enough stress on your body to stimulate improvement, you will have to go back to a reduced level and work up again.

The temptation to double up and push ahead is often greatest just when it is most dangerous—after an illness that was brought on by overtraining in the first place. This frequently occurs when someone is pushing for a particular level of conditioning or preparing for a big race. The runner feels great and is improving rapidly, but fails to take note of the signs of overwork. As a result he gets sick, fights with a cold or flu for a couple of weeks, perhaps trying to keep running part of the time.

Once the runner is over the cold, reserves will be depleted and some conditioning lost. Even if overtraining did not contribute to the illness, an attempt to make up for lost time will place great demands on the body just when it is worst equipped to meet them. It is important to return to base level conditioning—easy running at distances that feel right. If you take it easy at first, your conditioning will return fairly quickly. If you try to push too hard, you risk serious injury.

Stretching and Supplementary Exercises

Stretches and supplementary exercises are important aids

to the prevention of injuries, particularly for people vulnerable to certain overuse syndromes. Specific techniques are discussed later in the book and will not be covered in this chapter. But it should be noted that the regular stretching and strengthening of certain muscle groups is among the most basic means of staying healthy and pain-free. Flexibility and overall muscle tone are fundamental to good health, along with good cardiopulmonary conditioning. Running is a fine exercise for developing a healthy heart, lungs, and blood vessels, but it does nothing for certain other important muscle groups, like those of the abdomen.

Even worse, running tends to tighten many muscle groups that are already inflexible and shortened in American adults. Stretching on a regular basis is the best way to counteract these problems. The runner who gets in the habit of spending a few minutes a day stretching will become more flexible instead of tighter. Such stretching routines do not have to be time consuming, since they can usually be worked into your schedule sometime during the day. Stretching doesn't work up a sweat, so you don't have the constraints that apply to running. Nor do all your stretches have to be done at the same time of day. In fact, doing a little stretching is an excellent way to relax when you are under mental or physical stress or when you have been sitting or standing in one place for a long time. Work a regular stretching routine into your daily schedule. You'll enjoy it, and you'll be far less likely to get hurt.

CHAPTER 3

Minor Irritations and Maladies

THERE ARE a great many small problems that can beset runners, though some people are far more sensitive to them than others. Some of these annoyances, like blisters on the feet, are minor only if they are properly handled. Large blisters can be quite disabling, and the possibility of infection is serious. Good treatment, though, will prevent most blisters and keep others from becoming large. Other maladies, like stitches, are serious enough to those who suffer from them, but the threat they pose is to performance in a particular race rather than the basic ability to run, so they can't be placed in the same category as a knee injury or a ruptured tendon.

Chafing Problems

The serious runner soon learns to deal with whatever chafing problems may be encountered on daily runs. Usually some combination of adhesive tape (for protection) and petroleum jelly (for lubrication) will take care of any area except the feet. Runners who are a little overweight, for example, frequently encounter chafing between the thighs, and the area can become quite raw during a long run. A generous layer of petroleum jelly applied before the run will usually eliminate the difficulty.

Regular runners are more likely to have to deal with skin irritation on occasions when they are running farther than usual. Long-distance races cause the most problems, since you don't want to lose time by stopping to adjust your clothing. The usual trouble spots are at the elastic bands of your shorts; under the armpits, where the arms rub lightly against your sides; between your thighs; on the nipples, because of the rubbing of the shirt; and at the bottom of the bra front and around the rear hardware for women wearing bras. Where rubbing fabric causes the irritation, many people apply adhesive tape to the skin, so that the friction will be between the tape and the fabric. Some men use Band-Aids over their nipples, while others use Vaseline at the expense of large stains on their shirts. Petroleum jelly is best under the arms and between the thighs. Include a jar in your racing bag. Runners who put in enough training miles usually develop toughened skin and rarely have difficulty with chafing, except during the first few hot-weather runs of the year.

Blisters

Blisters on the feet can cause the runner real problems. They can be quite painful, particularly if you keep on running, raising large areas of skin and then breaking them open. The resultant sores are likely to take some time to heal; and since they will be at places where your shoes rub, they are likely to interfere with running for some time. Finally,

the possibility of infection from broken blisters, though unlikely, is dangerous enough to demand attention.

Blisters are one of the best possible examples of the adage
that an ounce of prevention is worth a pound of cure. It is
relatively easy to prevent blisters, but difficult to deal with
them once they have formed. Blisters on the feet are caused
by repeated mechanical shearing stress on the skin, which
gradually breaks down the tissue below, finally pulling the
skin free from the underlying flesh. Because of damage to the
cells and as protection against more friction, a cushion of
serum from the blood fills the cavity below the skin. Continued abrasion will usually result in a larger blister and finally in rupture of the skin, so that the blister becomes an
open sore. Sometimes the shearing action is transmitted
deeper into the flesh, and a blood blister forms at a deeper
level. Deep blood blisters usually occur when the affected
skin is deeply callused.

Prevention of blisters should begin when you buy your
shoes. Even if you plan to wear socks, it's a good idea to try
running shoes on barefoot and trot around the shop in them,
to determine any places where the shoes might irritate your
feet. Don't go by other people's recommendations or even
your own experience with the same model shoe. Every
pair is a little different, and one fold that occurs in a slightly
different place can be enough to raise blisters. Smooth surfaces are less likely to cause blisters than rough ones. Nylon
shoes are less apt to do so than leather ones. Though there
are many modifications you can make to shoes that are giving
you blisters, modern nylon running shoes should be adequate
from the day you buy them, requiring neither a breaking-in
period nor modifications before you go out and run a few
miles blister-free.

A good fit is important for preventing blisters and avoiding
other foot problems. A running shoe should fit over the socks

you'll normally wear with it so that it is snug but not constricting. There should be plenty of room around your toes, so that they won't jam against the front of the shoe when your feet swell up during a long, hot run or when you are running steep downhills. Your feet shouldn't slide around inside the shoes, and the sole should bend easily enough that the heel doesn't rub up and down. Be sure to bring along everything you wear in your shoes when you go to try a new pair on. Orthotics, insoles, and socks all affect the fit significantly.

If you are particularly prone to getting blisters, you should probably wear socks. Socks that fit well provide an extra layer in which shearing force can be dissipated without damaging your skin. Obviously, socks that ride down and bunch up inside your shoes are worse than useless. Ankle-length socks, short ones the same height as the shoe, and high ones that cover the calf are all used successfully by different people. Two light pairs can be worn to eliminate still more friction, a technique often adopted by climbers who wear heavy, stiff boots, but this should not normally be necessary with running shoes.

There are many schools of thought about material for socks. I prefer lightweight wool socks made from a very soft wool. Wool stays relatively springy and doesn't soften the skin so much when it is damp. Cotton is nice when it is dry, but it can be very abrasive and bunch up badly when it becomes soaked with perspiration or water. Tight nylon stretch socks make your feet hot and don't pass perspiration out very well, so it is best to avoid them. I find that bulked Orlon works well, though not as well as wool.

Shaking talcum or foot powder into your shoes before a run can help to prevent blisters by reducing friction for the first few miles of a run, though the powder will finally become soaked with perspiration. Some runners who have trouble with blisters like to put a large gob of petroleum jelly in each shoe before a long run. This method has the disadvantage of forming a barrier against the evaporation of moisture, but it works for many people.

One major cause of blisters that is neglected by many manufacturers is the arch cushion, usually made of bare sponge rubber. In many shoes the cushion provides so little support that it never rubs significantly. Some of the newer shoes are designed so that the cushion actually does give significant support to the arch, however, particularly for runners who pronate excessively. (Pronation is discussed in Chapter Eighteen.) This feature is a welcome improvement, but the designers have not followed it up by covering the cushions with nylon.

If you find that you are having trouble with friction from these cushions against the arch of your foot, the best solution is to cut a piece of smooth nylon material to the shape of the exposed portion of the cushion. (Mark the material and check the fit before cutting. It should extend a little way onto the insole.) Apply contact cement to the cushion and the bottom of the fabric piece, allow the glue to dry until it is no longer wet or sticky to the touch, and press the cloth against the cushion. Aim correctly the first time; contact cement sticks when it comes together, so if you align the cloth wrong, you'll have to rip it off and start over. To make sure that all the edges are held down completely, it's best to spread glue over an area in the shoe a little wider than the size of the cloth. Sprinkle talcum in the shoe after you are done to cover any sticky spots.

The most important rule for avoiding blisters is to stop when you first begin to feel uncomfortable friction on any part of your foot. You'll always feel some warning discomfort, but it won't be much longer before the blister forms.

Resist the temptation to run that extra mile. You'll regret it later. Stop and take off your shoe so that you can check the spot and see if there is any remedy. Red and irritated skin is a sure sign that a blister is not far off.

An irritated spot on your foot should be enough to send you home. There is always a strong urge to finish the run, but it is usually foolish and should be resisted. Getting in an extra five miles on one occasion is rarely worth the training that is likely to be lost later on. The worst situation arises when you have foot trouble in an important race. There are times when going on to finish is well worth the trouble it may cause, but you should weigh your desire to finish against the strong possibility that you won't be able to train for a couple of weeks. Be particularly hesitant if you have foot trouble early in a long race like a marathon. Your feet will be rubbed raw by the end.

During training runs it is never worth running any farther with an incipient blister than is necessary to get home. If nothing can be done to eliminate the irritation, you may want to walk home or even hitchhike to avoid getting blisters.

Usually blisters can be prevented by careful choice of shoes and socks, but people who still have difficulties may want to use other protective measures, particularly before a long race. Adhesive tape can be used to cover those parts of the feet that usually get blisters. Even better is *moleskin*, an adhesive-backed felt that can be purchased at drugstores. The feet can also be toughened in advance by applying a skin-toughening product, usually polyvinyl alcohol.

Treating Blisters

Irritated areas that have not yet formed blisters can be treated fairly easily. Leave the skin uncovered until your next run, since it will heal best if left alone. If you have another pair of shoes than the ones that caused the problem, it is best to wear them for a few days so that the skin can toughen. Otherwise, cover the entire area of the foot surrounding the irritation with moleskin.

The moleskin has several effects. It distributes the shearing stress over a wider area of skin, so that it is not localized at a small spot, while at the same time providing a smooth surface that may eliminate some friction. Leave the moleskin in place until it starts to come off, since pulling it off is hard on the skin.

Once a blister has formed, treatment should concentrate on eliminating all rubbing and pressure against the blistered skin. This is done by using moleskin to build a pad around the blister, so that pressure is transmitted to the surrounding skin. The larger the blister, the more difficult it will be to achieve this well enough to permit running. The usual technique is to cut a large pad of moleskin, cut a hole in the center the size of the blister, and apply the moleskin so that it surrounds the blister. Two layers of moleskin are sometimes necessary to relieve pressure, and it is usually best if one is smaller than the other, so that there is a gradual buildup of height on the area around the blister.

It is usually best to avoid lancing blisters unless it is impossible to relieve pressure on them any other way. Leaving the blister intact allows healing to progress without danger of infection. Large blisters and blisters on the toes sometimes require lancing as the only way to avoid having the shoes press on them. Lance the blister at one edge with a sterilized needle and press the fluid out. Then apply moleskin around the blister.

When a blister is too large for the pressure on it to be relieved with padding around the affected area, I prefer to cover the blister itself with Vaseline to reduce friction, put on a thin Telfa dressing (which will not stick to the wound), and cover the surrounding area with moleskin to relieve pressure. The whole dressing is then covered with another layer of moleskin to protect the dressing and the first layer of moleskin.

Before lancing a blister or dressing a broken blister it is important to wash your foot thoroughly and allow it to dry. Infection is especially dangerous in the foot, and it will greatly

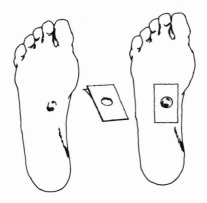

The best way to protect a blister that has already formed from further irritation is to use a large piece of moleskin (adhesive-backed felt) to cover the surrounding area, with a piece cut out of the center for the blister to protrude. Additional layers of moleskin can be used if necessary to provide enough cushioning.

prolong your recuperation period as well. Keep the area clean until it has healed. Use an antiseptic like aqueous zepharin if you like, but avoid antiseptics with red dye, which conceal the first signs of infection. If you are continuing to run, I would suggest that you wash your shoes also. None of this will make the foot a sterile area, but it will at least reduce the bacteria count near the wound.

If the blister is bad enough so that you can't help favoring your injured foot, regardless of protective padding and dressings, you should switch to another activity for a few days. It is easy to hurt your knees while favoring a blistered foot. When running with a moleskin dressing, allow for the possibility that it will begin to peel off; don't get too far from home and risk even worse abrasion. Run a circuit that stays within a mile or two of the house; or carry moleskin, scissors, and Vaseline along to repair your padding.

Calluses, Corns, and Warts

Calluses are protective layers of skin that form to insulate the underlying tissue from friction. As indicated in Chapter Eighteen, thick calluses may be a clue to foot weaknesses that put excessive pressure on some parts of the foot. Generally, calluses present no real problem if they are properly cared for, but a callus that is allowed to become too thick can transmit shearing stress to the tissue below and cause deep blood blisters. The hard callus may also crack, resulting in a sore. Keep calluses from thickening too much by filing them with pumice stone, and soften them by rubbing with petroleum jelly.

Corns and deep calluses may form over pressure points, usually the tops of the toes or under the heads of the metatarsal bones in the ball of the foot. The deep roots of these formations can press against nerves and be quite painful. Try to find the source of the pressure first. If it comes from a particular pair of shoes and cannot be corrected, throw the shoes away.

The pressure can sometimes be relieved by placing moleskin on the surrounding area with a hole cut out for the callus or corn. The top of the growth can be trimmed off if care is used. This will relieve some pressure. Cutting a hole at the appropriate spot in your shoe or insole will often relieve pressure. Chemical corn preparations damage too much surrounding skin and should not be used. A doctor can surgically remove the corn or callus fairly easily, but if you have recurrent problems in the same place, you may want to see a podiatrist to get at the cause. One good way to relieve pressure at points on the bottom of the foot is to buy Spenco insoles or make insoles from nylon-backed neoprene foam. Mark the spots that bear too much pressure carefully, and cut away foam from the bottom of the insole to create cavities there. The nylon layer on top is left intact to provide a smooth surface. Try the insoles and adjust the hollows until you are sure everything is right. Then glue the insoles in the shoes with latex or contact cement.

Warts are sometimes mistaken for corns, but they have a completely different structure and origin. They may form over a pressure point, but they often grow elsewhere as well. They are partially caused by a virus, but the entire process is not well understood. A wart can usually be distinguished from a corn by pressing and pinching. Warts are painful to pinching more than to pressure, because they are living growths, not just skin deposits. Corns are not sensitive to pinching. If you have problems with warts, see a physician.

Toenail Problems

Most nail difficulties can be avoided by keeping the toenails trimmed and buying shoes that fit well and are large enough. Nails can become badly bruised during a long run if they are too long and bang against the front of the shoe. The same injury can occur if the shoe is a little tight, pressing against the nail with each step. When you try on a pair of shoes, remember that your feet will expand significantly during a long run in hot weather. Buy shoes that have room in the toe but that don't permit your feet to slide forward too easily so that your foot will bang against the front when running downhill. Runners who use additional insoles or supports sometimes have difficulty finding shoes with enough toe room; but if you check several brands, you will usually find that some have much higher toes than others. Slits can also be cut in the shoes to relieve excessive pressure.

Severe banging of the nail against the shoe will cause a blackened nail and painful toe. This is not a serious injury,

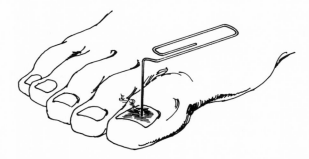

Bruised nails should usually be left alone to heal. If pain becomes intolerable from the pressure of bleeding below the nail, however, it can be relieved by drilling through the nail or burning a hole with a heated paper clip.

and the pain will disappear after a while. The purple that appears after the injury, later turning black, is caused by bleeding under the nail after repeated shearing stress. Much of the pain associated with this injury is caused by the pressure of the bleeding. Icing will help. If you want to relieve the pressure, this can be done fairly easily by drilling through the nail with a sharp awl or a tiny drill bit held between the fingers. The ones included in woodcarving sets are perfect. Relief of pressure can also be accomplished with a little more pain by heating the end of a bent paper clip on the stove and burning a hole through the nail. This gives the blood an escape route and will relieve much of the pain. The nail will take many months to grow out, and it will probably fall off after six months or so. This is of no real concern once the initial pain has disappeared.

Ingrown nails can be caused by improper trimming, pressure from shoes, or simply the shape of your foot. Daily care will usually prevent them from causing pain. It is usually best to file the point from any sharp corner, but let the nail grow out to prevent constant recurrence of the problem. A bit of cotton can be placed under the corner of the nail to reduce irritation. It should be replaced every day.

Athlete's Foot

Athlete's foot is a fungus infection of the foot, generally spread in showers and locker rooms used by many people, so it is naturally far more common among people exposed in this way. Many different varieties of fungi can be involved, but the problem is normally controlled fairly easily if it is vigorously treated. Good foot care usually will prevent contracting the infection at all.

After using public showers be sure to dry your feet completely, and use a fungicidal powder in your shoes. Fungi thrive in a damp environment and do not survive in a dry one, so everything you can do to keep your feet dry is helpful in preventing or curing athlete's foot. If you do catch a fungal growth in your feet, it will usually be signalled by itching and redness or blisters between the toes. Use a commercial preparation from the drugstore to treat the area, wear absorbent socks and change them frequently, use powder in your shoes, wear shoes that breathe well, and go barefoot when possible. You should see an improvement within a week. If the infection gets worse, see a doctor to avoid the possibility of complications from the bacterial infection of the open sores.

Stitches

Stitches are pains in the side of the abdomen. They are familiar to anyone who has ever tried to catch a bus after eating a heavy meal. Most runners experience them at one time or another, but some people are far more vulnerable than others. Stitches are not completely understood, though they seem to originate in a spasm of the diaphragm, the large muscular membrane between the abdominal and chest cavities, which pulls down to expand the lungs.

There is no universally applicable explanation for stitches, nor any infallible remedy. All one can do is mention some of the predisposing elements that often bring stitches on, and a few of the tricks that sometimes work to get rid of them. Breathing harder than you are used to is definitely a frequent cause of stitches. Like the other muscles of your body, the diaphragm has to be conditioned to various levels of work. You are likely to find that you get stitches more easily when you are racing or doing speed work. Starting too fast in a race is likely to bring on a stitch. In fact, just being tense during the first few miles is often enough to precipitate one. This is probably because you tighten your abdominal muscles and do most of your breathing with the chest. It helps to concentrate on deep, relaxed belly breathing.

Belly breathing is a definite help in preventing stitches. It may be that some parts of the diaphragm don't get an adequate blood supply when you breathe mainly with your chest, but whatever the reason, most runners find that concentrating on belly breathing helps to prevent stitches. You can often rid yourself of a stitch while still running by belly breathing and exhaling against some resistance, which helps to push the diaphragm down. The resistance can be supplied by breathing out through your nose, exhaling through partially closed lips, or by sighing, moaning, or rasping.

Stopping and doing a few stretching exercises will always get rid of a stitch, of course, but this won't make you very happy in a race, so if you plan to do any racing, you should practice getting rid of stitches while running. Nothing works all the time, but the techniques just mentioned will usually help.

Running downhill often brings on stitches. I think this is because one tends to tense the abdominal muscles as part of the cushioning action during fast downhill running. Concentrate on running with a fast, light stride, and belly breathe consciously whenever you run a long downhill.

Some runners find that stitches are associated with eating particular foods, which are evidently hard on their digestive systems. This may be due to gas accumulating in the digestive tract, causing pressure in the abdominal cavity. Certainly, anyone is more likely to get a stitch if he runs before a heavy meal has been completely digested. The lesson is obvious: If you must eat before an important race, eat only lightly, and only familiar foods that you know agree with you.

Shoulder and Upper Back Pains

Some tensing and pain in the shoulders and upper back are quite common during long runs, especially if you are straining a bit or if it is chilly. This is due to prolonged tension in the muscles of the upper body, particularly as you tire and have to concentrate more to maintain your pace. Such pains are a minor annoyance, though they can sometimes become chronic on long runs if you develop the habit of keeping some muscle tensed for a long period. It is worthwhile to learn to relax your upper body, both to avoid the minor irritation of shoulder pain and to make your style more economical. Tensed muscles are inefficient and are using oxygen and nutrients that would be better spent in forward propulsion.

Think about your upper body occasionally on long runs. Concentrate on relaxing each muscle in turn. It is often helpful to let your arms hang free and bounce for a few strides. I like to stretch my arms and swing them around every few miles without breaking my stride. This provides a pleasant relief and reduces fatigue and cramping of the upper body.

Numbness

Toward the end of a run that is long and hard enough to push your limits, numbness is fairly common in the hands and arms, and may extend even to your legs. The numbness in the arms seems to be due simply to a diversion of the bulk of the blood supply to the legs, as the body's reserves become exhausted. Numbness of the legs doesn't usually occur until well after you have passed the "wall" or "collapse point," the stage at which you involuntarily slow down radically.

These symptoms are not anything to worry about if you are in proper condition to run this far. It's worth noting, however, that some runners experience a drop in blood pressure after stopping when they have done an extended run, and this can cause fainting. This is an individual matter, but it is prudent to go through a short "cool down" period, walking or jogging a bit after finishing the run to keep the blood from pooling in the legs.

CHAPTER 4

Types of Injuries

T HERE ARE many ways to classify illnesses and injuries, depending on what one is trying to accomplish. Runners' maladies usually fall within a few fairly narrow categories, and most of them are not very common outside the field of sports medicine. A few injuries that can trouble runners are also common in the rest of the population. There is the usual run of traumatic injuries—those caused by violent physical forces. These may include a wide range of disorders, ranging from dog bites to the injuries inflicted when a runner is hit by a car. Sprained or broken ankles are always a possibility if you accidentally step into a hole or land badly while running on trails. By and large, though, running does not pose much of a danger of traumatic injuries—particularly when compared with contact sports like football and basketball, or even sports that require rapid changes of direction, like tennis.

Runners are also sometimes vulnerable to hazards from heat and cold. The dangers of running long distance races in hot weather can be quite significant, especially for runners who are poorly acclimated to the heat. Hot weather marathons have sometimes taken on the look of a battlefield, and deaths from heat stroke have occasionally resulted.

Separate chapters are devoted to most of these maladies later in the book, and particular attention is paid to those that pose some special danger to runners and to the ones like sprained ankles that might be aggravated by ill-advised running.

The special curse of the runner, though, is the group of injuries that are often called overuse injuries, because they result from stresses repeated thousands or even millions of times.

The occurrence of such overuse injuries should not surprise us. Even though our ancestors have run for millennia, they ran intermittently and on varied surfaces, often soft ones. We tend to run steadily at relatively fast speeds on hard surfaces. We often do so after many years of engaging in very little strenuous activity at all. Our feet are often deformed and weak from many years of wearing tight shoes and doing little walking.

Furthermore, though humans are excellent long distance runners, we still have some evolutionary problems associated with our upright stance. In nature's time scale for the evolution of higher animals, we haven't been up on our feet for a very long time at all, and there are still a few weaknesses in the system. We exacerbate these by the way we live.

Overuse is a fairly clear term, but one that covers a lot of ground. It does not take us to the real causes of a particular injury. Overuse injuries are typically frustrating because the origins are often difficult to understand. Their onset may be slow. They become incrementally worse without our really noticing their day-to-day progress. This is one of the reasons why runners will frequently sustain crippling injuries without ever doing much about them. There is no radical change that calls forth action—on some days the problem seems a little better, and we keep hoping it will go away. The response of this type of injury to treatment can be very slow, so that it is difficult to tell whether treatment is helping. This ambiguous response is further complicated, because when we finally start to feel better, we are likely to increase training and set the progress back.

To get some idea of the magnitude of the stress imposed on the legs and feet, consider a reasonably good runner who does marathons regularly but is not in the top class. He or she probably runs at least eighty miles a week. An average stride length might be about five feet, so our typical good runner takes about 84,480 running steps a week, and 4,392,960 a year. Each heel is hitting the ground well over two million times a year through running alone. Most top competitors will run even more than this. Any weak link in the leg or the foot of a runner is thus absorbing shock thousands of times a day. It isn't hard to see why the links sometimes give way.

These figures also show how much difference very small changes can make. If one side of the heel of your shoe is worn down a quarter-inch, your foot is being twisted slightly and your weight comes down incorrectly on the joints thousands of times a day. On the other hand, a little more cushioning in your shoes or slightly better alignment, multiplied by tens of thousands of repetitions a week, may often make enough difference to allow an injury to heal.

Causes of Overuse Injuries

Running involves a very complex series of body movements, with rather large forces being transmitted through the musculoskeletal system. Balance is fairly delicate throughout, since only one foot at a time is in contact with the ground and the body is airborne through a good deal of the stride. Running is in fact a series of linked jumps. Since the weight of the body and the propulsive force are transmitted through a single leg and foot at a time, a slight misalignment or poor support from a shoe can transmit imbalances up through the leg. Because the area of support is so small, rather large forces may have to be exerted by muscles anywhere from the foot to the spine to correct even minor imbalances.

Since the impact at each step is quite large compared with the normal demands of daily life, imbalances in the spine may also cause major difficulties to the runner, though they are dormant during less strenuous activities. The spine is as much an active part of running as the feet, because the hips and shoulders are rotating in opposite directions during each stride. The subtle shifts of balance that are necessary to keep the body's center of gravity over the foot striking the ground are also transmitted through the spine.

It is important for the runner to understand that few overuse injuries can be isolated to a single cause. Even when the injury is successfully treated by changing a single contributing factor, this may not mean that the only cause has been found. It may rather indicate that the restorative capacities of the body needed only a little help to tip the scale. The multiplicity of factors involved in many injuries should never be forgotten, because there is always a temptation to look for a single explanation. This tendency is as apparent in the medical profession as it is among runners. Looking for a single cause at a time is often a necessary approach to curing an injury, because the effects of a particular treatment can only be ascertained if it is used alone. Ultimately, however, a combination of remedies may be needed to allow the athlete to run without pain.

The complexity of the causes of running injuries often makes them difficult to diagnose and understand, but there is no way to avoid the dilemma. The very definition of a cause can be ambiguous. Shoes with inadequate cushioning for a particular runner who is training many miles on pavement are not really the *cause* of injuries, but changing to better shoes may well cure them. Similarly, a defect in foot structure or a rapid increase in mileage alone may not cause a knee injury, while the two put together do. Neither really causes the injury; it is the combination that is not tolerated.

Both the runner and the doctor are thus often feeling about in the dark. A doctor may know that on some occasions a particular foot deformity or spinal irregularity is associated with the same symptoms a runner exhibits, prescribing a certain course of treatment. If other causes are also contributing, however, the single remedy may not be enough to reverse the problem, especially in advanced stages. Often several approaches are needed at the same time.

Some of the most common causes of overuse injuries are:

1. *Improper training technique.* There are many mistakes that one can make. The most important (and this is impossible to overemphasize) is overtraining—increasing the work load beyond the capacity of the body to adapt. Many other cases are secondary to this one and would not result in injury were they not combined with overtraining. Overtraining injuries can result from increasing distance, speed, hills, heat, hard surfaces, or any

combination of these. They can also follow from simply trying to maintain the same load when other pressures are making demands—when you have put on weight, or when you are ill or run-down. *Overtraining is the single greatest cause of injuries.*

2. *Tightness and inflexibility* because of the effects of training and failure to stretch. The obvious way to eliminate this cause of injury is to stretch regularly. Muscles are also usually rather tight before you have properly warmed up, and starting off at high speed is a good way to pull a muscle, especially in cold weather and early in the morning.

3. *Imbalanced muscular development.* Studies have demonstrated that runners with major differences in strength or flexibility between opposing muscle groups will usually pull or tear one of the affected sinews. Since most types of running develop the muscles along the back of the legs, exercises for the opposing muscles are important. Balance between the muscles of the two legs also helps prevent injuries, and abdominal exercises help to prevent lower back pain. Runners with back problems often need special exercises to help the spine withstand the stresses imposed by running. Runners with a chronic susceptibility to muscle pulls and strains can usually eliminate the problem with a suitable combination of stretching and exercising.

4. *Poorly chosen or badly maintained shoes.* Shoes may cause difficulties themselves, particularly if they are allowed to wear unevenly. They may aggravate other problems by combining with foot abnormalities, training techniques, and other factors to cause an injury. Shoes do not usually *cause* injuries, but a better choice of shoes will often help *prevent* them by providing bet-

ter cushioning or support and perhaps compensating for mild foot abnormalities. Because people have different feet and varying needs, there is no one "best" shoe. The perfect shoe for me might be a very poor choice for you. Careful selection and maintenance of shoes can be an important factor in the prevention and healing of injuries.

5. *Structural abnormalities of the feet, legs, or back.* These are the causes of the most intractable runners' injuries, *but not the majority of injuries.* Remember that overtraining is often the most immediate cause even of injuries to which structural problems contribute. A great deal has been learned in recent years about the correction of injuries caused by structural problems, both by orthopedic specialists and by podiatrists (foot doctors). Structural imperfections that are very minor and will cause no symptoms in daily life will often generate enough distorting forces under the additional stress of running to result in injuries. These do not necessarily show up at the part of the body that is causing the trouble. Abnormalities of the spine may manifest themselves through pains in the legs, while improper foot structure may cause lower back pain. The problem for runners is made more difficult by the war between the specialists and the lack of widespread understanding of running ailments in the medical profession.

Very often the injuries caused by structural abnormalities can be controlled with proper treatment. This may involve stretches, special exercises, or rest followed by carefully designed training and therapy. It may require modifications to the shoes or special inserts called orthotics to balance the foot. Surgery may also be necessary, but not often. There are also a few people with structural difficulties that make running impossible or inadvisable, but they are rare.

Distinguishing Between Types of Injuries

The first step in understanding an injury is often to classify the type. A great deal can be determined from fairly simple information. You should keep a record of symptoms, either in your running diary or separately. This is a worthwhile habit to cultivate, because a record of symptoms is important to the diagnosis if the injury gets worse later on. Whether or not you are planning to go to a doctor immediately, writing things down is useful. Otherwise, you will find later on that you have only the vaguest recollection of when the symptoms actually began—two weeks ago? a month? two months?

Another reason that an accurate record is important is that it enables you to relate the injury to your activity at the time. Was it precipitated by a hard hill training session or by the purchase of a new pair of shoes? The correlation of the onset of the injury with your training at the time is crucial. If the beginnings of the injury correspond to a period of heavy training, there is good reason to suspect that that is the cause.

Be sure to keep a very accurate record of everything related to your running when you are fighting off an injury. It is often surprising how after suffering from a problem for a month you can find some clue that will suggest a solution. For example, I once developed bursitis in my heel because of the pressure from a particular pair of shoes. I did not suspect the shoes at first, because I had worn them for some time whenever I went on trail runs. This apparently had not irritated my foot enough to cause any trouble. When another pair of shoes wore out and I started to use these all the time, though, I began to have trouble, which I thought at first was Achilles tendonitis. When the actual diagnosis finally occurred to me, it was confirmed by the timing of the injury. It began to improve as soon as I changed shoes.

Injuries may turn out to be related to a change in running surface, wearing down shoe heels to a certain level, and so on. A diary can speed the diagnosis of an injury by weeks, reducing the potential seriousness. If a leg pain turns out to be a minor muscle pull and goes away within a few days, the entry noting the injury is forgotten, but if the pain gets worse the record is useful. It takes only a few seconds to note your runs and any problems you've encountered in a small notebook. For the serious runner such a diary is also invaluable in planning training, since you can go back to find out what training patterns brought the best results.

The type of pain, the mode of onset, and the times when it appears are particularly important. A sharp pain that comes on suddenly in the body of a muscle immediately leads one to suspect a pulled muscle. The diagnosis can often be made from a distance. You can see someone doing speed work on the track or running in a race suddenly pull up short or start to limp, grabbing the back of the thigh. The diagnosis is a torn hamstring. Other injuries come on slowly and may be deeper and vaguer pains. Some injuries hurt in the morning or in bed rather than when you are actually running.

Strains of the muscles and some tendons usually come on quite suddenly, though the underlying causes may have been building up for some time. Sprains—tearing the ligaments in the joints—are also sudden in onset, but these are usually more obvious in their cause, resulting from an accidental misstep or other abnormal force in a direction outside the normal range of motion. Pain with sprains is usually fairly sharp.

Other types of injuries begin almost imperceptibly, gradually becoming worse by degrees, and may include either sharp pains or aching ones, local or generalized. Many of the chronic injuries that plague runners are of this type, starting out as a minor annoyance or a slight twinge, but gradually progressing until they are incapacitating. This is the sort of injury where it is particularly helpful to keep careful notes. Don't be a hypochondriac, but pay careful attention to what is going on.

Make a careful note of the location of the pain. As an injury progresses, pain frequently is felt over a much wider area, but this does not necessarily mean that the injury is any larger. The pain is often "referred," felt in a different place than the actual trouble. Pain may be referred from the onset, especially when it is due to nerve irritation. This means the location of the pain is not *always* the same as the location of the trouble. More often, though, the first signs are at the site of the actual injury. This is easy to forget when the injury gets worse, because initial troubles may be minor. Thus a case of shinsplints may start out mildly, and by the time they are bad enough to really cause trouble, pain may be felt all the way through the knee. The knee is not really involved, and noting the origin of the trouble is a great help in treating it later on.

Some pains are of the "shooting" type, running along a particular pathway. An example is a burning-type pain running from the lower back or deep in the hip down the leg to the big toe. This sort of finding can be quite significant, because the pain follows the course of a nerve, and the actual trouble may lie anywhere along the nerve. Nerve problems can be quite difficult, and they receive a lot of attention in the literature, but they are fortunately quite uncommon among runners. The nerve difficulties that do occur are most frequently found in the foot, a subject discussed later in the book. Sciatica—irritation of the nerve running from the lower back and deep in the hip down to the big toe—can be quite intractable, but is rather rare in runners. Many cases diagnosed as sciatica have actually turned out to be muscle pulls in the hip.

Overtraining vs. Structural Problems

One of the most important distinctions in dealing with an injury is between one that is caused primarily by structural difficulties and one that is mainly a result of overtraining. As stated earlier in the chapter, a few injuries result purely from one cause or the other, but the distinction is still an important one. Serious structural problems will often manifest themselves at a particular level of stress, no matter how carefully the athlete builds up to that level. This sort of difficulty may strike a runner soon after the beginning of speed training, no matter how cautiously he has prepared for it. It may begin to cause trouble at a particular weekly mileage, regardless of how slowly the runner increases to that figure.

This is another point at which most runners go astray in diagnosing their own troubles, leaping immediately to fantasies about strange and exotic foot disorders when their real difficulties lie in their training schedules. More information on specific symptoms and maladies will be included in later chapters of the book, but this is where we encounter the most important rule to follow in considering your injuries: ALWAYS LOOK FOR THE MOST OBVIOUS EXPLANATIONS AND SOLUTIONS FIRST. CONSIDER THE STRANGE AND UNUSUAL POSSIBILITIES ONLY IF THE MOST LIKELY DIAGNOSIS PROVES TO BE WRONG. When you start to get the sniffles, you assume that you have a cold or hay fever. It *might* be the start of some rare and exotic disease, but the intelligent person presumes it is a cold until there is some good reason to suspect otherwise. If you apply the same logic to your running injuries, you'll find the solutions to your problems a lot more quickly. You will also be less likely to hurt yourself further.

If you sustain an injury you should guess first that you have overtrained. Instead, most runners will continue to try to train at the same pace and will look for structural causes. The newer shoes and the latest accomplishments of podiatric medicine are a wonderful thing, but they won't save you from your own excessive zeal. The best rule to follow when you get hurt is to back off on your training immediately, do the appropriate stretches, exercises, and warm-ups religiously, and increase the work load again only when you are well on the way to recovery. *And* increase training more slowly the next time around. (Some types of injuries, discussed more fully later in the book, may call for a complete layoff for a time.)

Look for structural problems only when you have ruled out other possibilities. If you have difficulties every time you increase stress to a certain level, regardless of how slowly and carefully you do it, your root problems may be structural. A serious competitor may also require the help of a podiatrist or orthopedist to work at the level necessary to reach his maximum potential. This is because of the very high level of stress being placed on all of the joints and muscles of the lower body. It is far more common, however, for someone twenty pounds overweight to increase his work load suddenly and to develop knee problems. He may also have minor weaknesses in his feet, but the *primary* cause of the injury is overstress. The most important treatment is not orthotics, but more sensible training.

Strains and Sprains

A strain is an injury to the structure of a muscle-tendon unit. Tendons are the fibrous bands that usually connect a muscle to the bone. Some muscles attach directly to bone, but most grade into tendonous tissue at each end before inserting into a bone. Unlike the muscle itself, the tendon has no power to contract, and its function is to connect the muscle and bone. Muscle-tendon units normally pass between the bones on either side of a joint. The purpose of the muscle is to pull the bones so that the joint bends in the direction of the muscle contraction. Some muscle-tendon units span two joints. Since a muscle and tendon unit extends over a joint, it may be vulnerable to overextension and damage when the joint is bent in the other direction, especially if the structure is tight, so that it is stretched nearly to the limit during normal motion of the joint.

Muscles are capable of exerting force only by contracting. During contraction individual muscle fibers shorten. The muscle cannot exert an extension force. Instead, a corresponding muscle on the other side of the joint must contract to pull the joint in the opposite direction. There are thus always at least two muscle-tendon structures associated with each moving joint. Often there are many more, especially for joints with complex three-dimensional motion like the hip joints.

Tearing of the muscle or tendon is called a *strain*. Three degrees of severity are recognized. First-degree strains involve tearing of only a small percentage of the fibers. Second-degree injuries involve tearing of a significant number of fibers, but not complete rupture, while third-degree injuries are those where the muscle or tendon is completely torn apart. Reliable diagnosis cannot be made until twenty-four hours after the injury, and is discussed in Chapter Fourteen.

Sprains are injuries to the ligaments surrounding the joints. There is a good deal of confusion between ligaments, tendons, and cartilage. The tendons have already been defined. They do not form parts of the joints, though they often extend over them. Ligaments are fibrous bands of tissue that connect bone to bone, holding the two halves of a joint together. They are relatively inflexible, so they can be easily and seriously torn if the joint is bent beyond its normal range.

Sprains are classified using the same system as strains, and they also require twenty-four hours before an accurate assessment of the extent of damage can be made. It should be noted that the strength of the ligament is not usually relied on to hold the joint together. The structure of the joint itself and the tension of the surrounding muscles and tendons are usually sufficient to maintain normal alignment. The ligaments act mainly to prevent excessive movement. One reason that sprains are more likely when you are tired is that the fatigued muscles may not be able to withstand normal sideways forces, so they may give way and allow all your body weight to fall on the ligaments. This is particularly dangerous to those with previous joint damage, whose ligaments may not be able to withstand the force.

Cartilage is a smooth, slippery, tough material that forms pads within some joints. It is designed to pad and lubricate the movement of the joint. If the pad of cartilage becomes rough or torn, however, it may actually interfere with joint motion rather than aid it. This is why orthopedic surgeons sometimes remove cartilage from the knee to relieve certain types of injuries, an operation that is usually effective. Cartilage can be damaged when the joint itself is injured. In this case it often heals with a rough surface that may cause trouble later on. Arthritis may also cause the cartilage to become rough, though for many sufferers running has improved this condition. Cartilage also sometimes tears from a seemingly minor force, for reasons not completely understood. Joint injuries where cartilage damage is suspected should always be examined by a qualified orthopedist. Proper diagnosis requires elaborate tests, and surgery is sometimes required.

Damage to the Tendons and Their Sheaths

The tendons are among the more vulnerable structures in runners, both because of tight muscle-tendon groups and because of the rubbing of the tendons over joints during running. Because of the repetitious nature of running, any motion that irritates a tendon even slightly can result in major inflammation after hundreds of thousands of cycles. Structural abnormalities can cause this type of irritation, and they can also put abnormal strain on the tendons if the foot, leg, or back is somewhat out of alignment, so that the muscles and tendons have to strain to maintain balance and normal motion.

Tendonitis is the irritation or inflammation of a tendon. Treatment and correction should take place as soon as it is recognized, since injuries to the tendons become more intractable the longer they are left untended. If the tendon is torn, failure to treat the tendonitis prevents healing of the fibers already torn and may lead to further damage. The sheath of an injured tendon may thicken, and this may cause pressure and added friction between the tendon and the sheath later on, so that there is a chronic condition. Furthermore, additional damage will mean that more scar tissue will form during healing, making the whole tendon tighter and weaker, so that future injuries become more likely.

Tenosynovitis is an inflammation of the tendon sheath or the sliding surface between the tendon and the sheath. Tendonitis and tenosynovitis have related causes and symptoms, and separation of the two may be difficult, as mentioned below.

There is some controversy among doctors over the relative frequency of various forms of tendonitis and tenosynovitis. This argument is of some consequence to the runner, because treatment may well depend on whether one believes that there has been much tearing of fibers within the tendon. Dr. William Clancy of the University of Wisconsin, who has probably had as much experience with the problem as anyone, maintains that most injuries in training, especially in the Achilles tendon (heel cord), are to the tissues of the tendon itself, not to the sheath. He feels that the symptoms of tendonitis normally mean there has been tearing of the fibers of the tendon and should be treated that way. He feels that tenosynovitis usually occurs only when the tendon rubs over a heel spur or similar irritating structure.

The symptoms of tendonitis include generalized pain in the area of the tendon, often worst in the morning when the muscles are stiff and haven't been used for a while, and sometimes occurring at night in bed. Stress on the tendon will increase the pain. With an Achilles tendon, for example, jumping up and down on tiptoes will be painful or impossible. With the Achilles tendon it is generally possible to locate the exact site of the injury by pinching the tendon between two fingers, starting at one end and moving slowly toward the other. Pinching along most of the length of the tendon should not produce much pain, but at the location of the injury it will be very noticeable. This test will usually separate tendonitis of the Achilles from tenosynovitis and bursitis (see below).

Injuries to the Bones

The most obvious bone injuries are those resulting from some sort of a bad slip, which can cause a *fracture*. Severe injuries of the knees and ankles should normally be evaluated by a physician to be sure there is no fracture. Runners also sometimes break small bones in the foot by stepping in holes or on rocks. Fractures in the foot occur most often to the metatarsals, the long bones running out to the toes along the top of the foot.

Most troublesome to runners are overuse injuries to the bones, which occur for the same reasons as other overuse injuries—repeated stress over a period of time, particularly during hard training or as a result of structural problems. The bones can fatigue much like a piece of wire or sheet metal being bent back and forth and gradually developing cracks. These fatigue cracks are called *stress fractures*.

Stress fractures can be difficult to diagnose, because they usually will not show up on X rays until weeks after their occurrence. They can occur in almost any bone from the spine down, but they are most common in the metatarsals, in the fibula (the outside bone of the lower leg), especially near the ankle, in the tibia (the inside bone of the lower leg), and less frequently in the heel bones and hips. Stress fractures are accompanied by generalized pain of a deep aching type. There will often be swelling, redness, and puffiness over the area of the stress fracture. It may be possible to locate the injury by pressing on the bone. This is particularly useful for stress fractures along the tibia, since it can be difficult to distinguish a stress fracture from shinsplints. If one spot along the crest of the bone is sensitive to pressure, a stress fracture is indicated. Generalized sensitivity all along the crest for some distance is indicative of the muscle strain syndrome properly termed *shinsplints*.

It is possible for the muscle or tendon to pull free at the point of attachment by tearing off a piece of bone. When an injury similar to a muscle pull occurs and a deep pain seems to come from around the bone, a physician should be consulted and X rays should be taken. The tendon may have torn completely where it inserts in the bone, or bone fragments may have been pulled loose. Either injury is serious. *Bone avulsion* is most common where the hamstrings insert in the hip; a deep pain will be felt under the buttocks. More rarely, a pain deep inside the groin in the hip area may occur when one of the quadriceps muscles pulls loose.

This type of injury can be particularly serious in adolescents, because bone can be pulled loose at the growth centers. The growth of the bone may be arrested unless the injury receives proper treatment. The most common such injury is felt at the belt line, when the sartorius muscle pulls bone loose from the growth plate. Injuries that cause pain near the bones in young people should receive the attention of a doctor.

Bursitis

Bursae are fluid-filled sacs placed under some tendons and ligaments where they cross joints. They are designed to act as pads, to cushion shock and ease the motion of the tendon. These bursae sometimes become inflamed themselves, causing pain and limiting motion. Inflammation can be caused by excessive pressure from the moving tendon, external pressure, or cold. It sometimes flares up for reasons that are not well understood. Shoulder bursitis can bother runners in cold weather if they become chilled, but the usual problem spots for runners are in the heel, on the outside of the knee, and on the outside of the lower hip.

Bursitis can occur in conjunction with tendonitis, especially in the heel, and it is important not to ignore possible tendon damage. Symptoms are similar but can usually be separated. Diagnosis and treatment are discussed in Chapter Six.

Heel Bumps and Spurs

Prolonged irritation and inflammation of the bursae either at the back or bottom of the heel will eventually stimulate the growth first of fibrous tissue and then of a bony protrusion at the affected spot. A growth on the back of the heel in the Achilles region is generally referred to as a *runner's bump*, while a growth on the bottom of the heel is called a *heel spur*. The first is generally the result of chronic tendon irritation and bursitis in the heel. Heel spurs result from a similar condition at the back of the arch, because of irritation of the *plantar fascia*, bands of tissue that extend from the heel bone across the arch like a bowstring.

Clearly, the best treatment for those bony protrusions is prevention, by treating the initial irritation immediately. These problems tend to become more and more aggravated, because once a bump or a spur forms, it further inflames the Achilles or the plantar fascia, sometimes even sawing through tissue. The basic causes may include all the conditions that precipitate tendonitis or bursitis, but they usually have their root in structural defects of the feet or legs. Foot supports will probably be required as part of a successful treatment. If they are allowed to grow too large, heel bumps and spurs may require surgical removal, but the underlying causes still have to be treated or the whole syndrome can be expected to repeat itself.

Similar growths and bumps can occur over other bones as a result of pressure and irritation or earlier traumatic injuries. Bumps caused by chronic irritation should be relieved by either shoe modifications or appropriate supports for the foot. Those bumps caused by earlier injuries sometimes require treatment by a podiatrist or orthopedist and may need to be surgically removed if they are too troublesome.

Softening of the Kneecap

A great many problems can occur in the knee, which is probably the most common source of trouble for runners. These will be considered in detail in a later chapter, because it is important to look at the mechanics of the leg and foot to understand them. They include tendonitis, bursitis, and a host of troubles connected with old knee injuries. One of the diseases of the knee that can affect runners is *chondromalacia of the patella*, softening of the cartilage on the back surface of the kneecap. Pain is felt immediately under the kneecap, often after sitting for some time and while climbing stairs. More precise tests are discussed later in the book to distinguish chondromalacia from some of the other common knee problems. Chondromalacia is usually due to mechanical causes, and it can generally be treated successfully with a combination of techniques including support of the feet.

Other Foot Problems

Besides stress fractures, bursitis, and heel bumps and spurs, the feet are subject to numerous maladies. Most of them are fortunately rather uncommon in runners. This is interesting, since there are probably more structural defects in the feet than in any other part of the running anatomy. Injuries caused by these defects, however, often show up in the knees and elsewhere in the legs. There are a number of fairly obvious deformities of the foot that can cause difficulties for runners. Because of their exotic nature and the clear advisability of consulting a podiatrist, they will not be considered in detail in this book.

Later chapters on the mechanics of the foot show some of the overuse injuries that can be caused by even subtle defects in foot structure. It is obvious that more radical departures from normal structure have the potential to cause major difficulties. Common sense suggests consulting a specialist if you have unusual feet and develop injuries. A very high and rigid arch can be one of the most difficult of structural defects and is frequently associated with Achilles problems, pain on the outside of the knee, heel spurs and bumps, and difficulties with the arch.

Strain of the arch has been mentioned briefly in connection with heel spurs. Those bands of ligamentlike tissue called the plantar fascia run from the heel bone to the ball of the foot and help support the arch. These can become painful or become torn by excessive stress. Such difficulties are often associated with mechanical problems in the foot, so treatment will be discussed in Chapter Eighteen.

Bruises on the heel can be caused by stepping on stones, and they are painful. They take a long time to heal and are best treated with padding around the bruised area. It is important, however, to distinguish between a bruise and a strain at the point where the plantar fascia join the heel bone, since the latter can result in further strain, bursitis, and heel spurs.

Pains between the metatarsals or the toe joints, especially if they are associated with nodes or lumps, can be due to *trapped or inflamed nerves.* So can other unexplained and increasing pain in the foot. These difficulties are not too common, but they should prompt you to visit a podiatrist if they fail to clear up in a reasonable amount of time.

CHAPTER 5

Training Without Injuries

T HE TITLE of this book, *Running Without Pain*, is serious, even though much of the rest of the book is devoted to a catalogue of injuries. Every serious runner who keeps going for a long time will experience some injuries, but I believe that if you apply the same diligence to preventing injuries and nipping them in the bud that you do your training schedule, you will probably be able to avoid serious pain and long layoffs. A sudden onset of catastrophic injuries is really quite unusual. One case history after another shows the same regular collection of patterns. Most runners have ample warning of injuries in their beginning stages—they just don't pay attention.

Common precursors to serious injury are the attempts to train hard continuously, to make up for lost conditioning time by working twice as hard, and to race at top effort too often, especially over long distances. Finally, there is the matter of stretching and supplementary exercises. Almost everyone pays lip service to these principles now, but I doubt that even a quarter of the serious runners in the country act on them.

The basic principles for injury prevention have already been covered in Chapter Two, and this chapter will concentrate on the practical application of these techniques by serious runners. The most fundamental rule is to watch seriously for signs of overstress and to heed them. Whatever kind of runner you are—recreational, age-group racer, noncompetitive marathoner, pack runner, or serious international contender—it is vital to recognize that your long-term satisfaction with running is going to be dependent on the way you treat your body. Pushing regularly over the fine line that defines overstress will finally result in more setbacks than advances. Later in the chapter we will also consider choice of shoes, maintenance, and repair.

Base Training

The debates over training techniques—long- or slow-distance, tempo or interval, quality vs. quantity—will undoubtedly continue to rage on for a long time in the future, as they have in the past. Many of the arguments turn out to revolve around semantics more than around substance, anyway, when the actual programs involved are studied. The difference in the responses of individuals and the psychological factors involved will always introduce large doses of uncertainty, no matter what the formula. Several important elements of any training program seem to be clearly important for those who want to avoid injury, however, especially for older runners.

One is the principle of slowly building up your level of

base training. It is important to distinguish periods of base training from either racing (or the noncompetitive equivalent) or sharpening prior to hard racing. *Racing is not training.* Training builds up reserves, making you a little stronger each day. Racing, if it is done hard and fast, taps those reserves. In the long run it does not strengthen you. It's like withdrawing money from a bank, which you've deposited bit by bit during training. If you try to keep withdrawing more often than you deposit, especially in large quantities, you'll finally deplete your reserves completely.

Beginners improve rapidly in both their capacity for distance training and their speed, even during base training; and this is likely to build up unrealistic expectations in those who have been running just a few years. You can continue to improve over time, but the rate of betterment is bound to decrease. The dedicated runner has to be satisfied with continuing good health and with small improvements; the days of the big breakthroughs are over. For those who have run since adolescence, improvement may not even be possible except by finding new areas of running.

A beginner who progresses from two miles at a twelve-minute pace to the marathon at six-minute miles during a period of two or three years will never experience that incredible conditioning rise again. He or she is probably close to the limits that can be tolerated without breakdown. Further improvements, if any, have to be approached carefully if injury is to be avoided.

Base training should be just that. You should not make daily attempts to run a little faster or to call out the last ounce of stamina your body possesses. You should finish most of your base training runs feeling fairly fresh. Your speed and distance may improve, but the process should be slow and steady. If you do speed work during base training, it should be low-key, designed to help you improve your overall pace a little, but not to run as fast as you possibly can over long distances.

Save your heavy and regular interval or speed sessions for the sharpening period before you intend to peak for a big race or a season. Remember that you cannot maintain peak form all the time. There will be highs and lows, and if you plan them you will race better when you want to and be less likely to hurt yourself.

This does not mean you should run nothing but long, slow distance. The work you are doing depends not only on your pace and mileage, but also on your past training and ability. An eight-minute pace is hard work for one runner and very slow for another. The point is that a lot of training at a *relatively* easy pace is essential if you want to go out some of the time to run hard intervals and, later, to race hard. The moderate running is what builds up the stamina and the mechanical strength in your body to withstand the pushes. To do so, the load has to be moderate as determined by the reactions of your body *now,* not moderate according to your preconceived notions of what you should be doing.

Racing

Tom Osler has pointed out that while running itself is good for us, long-distance racing is a form of self-abuse. Training runs leave you stronger after a day or two of rest. No one is stronger the day after a hard marathon. Even superdistance specialists who can stand incredible abuse are able to run back-to-back marathons or ultramarathons only by pacing themselves slower than they otherwise would. During hard distance races, especially those over twenty miles, you have to reach deep into your body's reserves. Do it too often and you will break down. Shorter races are not quite so hard on you, but running even ten kilometers as hard as you can will significantly tap your reserves. If you run enough 10,000-meter races in a row at your maximum level of effort, you will find yourself going stale. If you continue to race hard after that, you'll get hurt.

No formula will substitute for consciousness of your own body and watching for signs of overwork. Everyone needs a different amount of base training to be able to race a certain distance, and there will be variations in each individual from one time to another. At *a minimum*, however, you should expect to put in ten training miles for every mile raced. Usually, more will be required to race consistently and well without overstressing the body. For marathons and ultramarathons, training mileage should be much higher. These figures refer to serious racing. If you go out and run a ten-mile race every weekend simply as a fast workout, without even approaching your potential or working hard, it is really a training run in a race setting. Don't kid yourself, though. A lot of runners participate in too many races, do poorly, and pass the signs of overtraining off by calling the race a "training" run.

The signs of overtraining listed in Chapter Two should be your guide during a racing session. If you show signs of overwork, drop back to base training. You won't do yourself or your performance any good by pushing forward in spite of the warnings. As a matter of good training practice, your performance should be fairly predictable. If you find yourself doing well in training runs or insignificant races and fading in races where you wanted to do well, you are not planning your base training and peaking properly. Peaks and stale periods will occur; and if you ignore the facts and try to train at your best level all the time, the extra spark will rarely be there when you want it.

Shoes

One of the really major advances in injury prevention for runners has taken place during the last few years with the improvements in training shoe design. Since running shoes have become a big business, there has been a real incentive toward competition in design, especially with injured runners coming to the realization that they need shoes to protect and support their feet, not just the latest hot racing shoes worn by current stars.

Podiatrists working with running injuries have discovered that mechanical imbalances that will cause injury during tens of thousands of miles of training are not the exception; they are the rule. The make-or-break styles of training and coaching of years ago selected runners with relatively stable feet simply by eliminating the others before they had become good enough to be noticed. Even so, many great competitors were forced to retire by injuries that could be prevented today. Wearing lightweight track shoes with no arch support at all, any runner with an unstable foot will begin having an intolerable number of injuries at a very early stage of training. This would be even truer today, because of the very high training mileage required of most top racers.

A runner with a light stride and a stable foot may be able to run in excess of a hundred miles a week in shoes that meet only minimal requirements: proper fit, a little cushioning at the heel and ball of the foot, and flexibility in the forefoot area. Most runners need a lot more than that to be able to run the roads every day without injury; their feet need good cushioning and support.

This difference is worth reflecting on, because there is a lesson in it. People's feet are not the same. The ideal shoe for me may not be ideal for you. In fact, I have to make modifications in many stock shoes to get the support I need from them. Some factors, like the amount of cushioning provided, are relatively straightforward, while others are quite variable. Flared soles, for example, provide extra stability along with good cushioning that is beneficial to many runners; but they flatten the feet too suddenly for other runners, causing ankle pain.

Some factors in shoe design can be considered as generally desirable, while others will be needed by some people and irrelevant to others. Still other features will be of benefit to

The construction of a good running shoe. The interior should be smooth so that the skin is not irritated, and the shoe should support your foot well. The suitability of different shoes varies with the foot of the individual. The Achilles padding sometimes irritates more than it protects. If it does, cut it off. The heel counter must hold your heel firmly, especially for running on rough trails. If you have Achilles problems, try a shoe with a high heel wedge. Get good shoes, especially if you have injuries. Cheap shoes usually have poor padding in the soles; the materials are often hard as a rock.

many runners and undesirable to a lot of others. This is not an unmanageable situation. There are enough runners now so that it is perfectly reasonable to expect to be able to buy shoes off the shelf that include certain mild corrections and support for different foot types.

Podiatrists frequently object that this is impossible, because of the incredible variation in people's feet. There is truth in this assertion, and quite a few runners will have to use custom-fitted plastic inserts to obtain satisfactory support for pain-free running. But many runners have minor foot weaknesses that can be adequately remedied with a little help from the shoe manufacturers or makers of mass-produced supports. It is certainly more useful to have several shoes with varied supports to try on in the shop than to have six brands with no difference except in their stripe patterns.

Most of the readers of this book are already familiar with running shoes, so I will not attempt to review the obvious elements of shoe design. Nylon has become the standard material for uppers, except for shoes that will be worn a lot in sloppy weather. Leather has some advantages in slush and mud, providing it is regularly treated with preservatives so that it doesn't develop hard spots. Sole patterns vary widely, but the main choice is between conventional embossed designs and the various copies of Nike's Waffle tread. There are advantages to each. Medical authorities differ on the importance of tread design in the prevention of injuries. I have spoken with a couple of podiatrists specializing in running injuries who believe that the Waffle-type sole offers no real advantages and has several problems. Others claim that the slight lateral give in this type of tread is significant in prevention of injuries, apart from the cushioning effect. Because the protrusions will deform sideways, the shoe can slide or turn slightly after landing, and this yielding quality may be significant in reducing stress on the legs.

There are also a few disadvantages to the Waffle-type sole from the point of view of injury prevention. They wear more quickly at the landing and takeoff areas, and sole wear can be a major cause of injury if allowed to go unchecked. For those runners who wear out parts of their soles very quickly, this means either that more time be spent on maintaining the tread or that resoling must be done more frequently. This is not an insignificant point, since some of us can wear down the protrusions on one side of the heel in a couple of long runs. That is why many of the makers of this type of sole are now molding special solid areas into the points of highest wear. Related to this problem is the fact that the Waffle-type soles are not as easy to maintain with glue guns (see below).

More important than tread design are the areas of cushioning, support, and flexibility. A lot of cushioning is desirable in training shoes. Our bodies were designed to run on soft surfaces rather than pavement, and the function of cushioning in shoes is to introduce a little give into the hard roads we usually run on. Serious racers may not want too much softness in their racing shoes, since some energy is dissipated, but this is not a concern in training shoes. For most of us, it is not really important for racing either. Shoe weight makes a difference, but the extra forward momentum that can be gained by decreasing cushioning should not concern most runners. Unless you are planning on competing seriously in the next Olympic Trials, the few seconds you might gain are not worth the risk of injury.

Cushioning is important both in the heel and the ball of the foot, in different degrees, depending on your running style. Most distance runners land on their heels, so this is the most important location for cushioning. Those who slap their feet down hard, drive off the forefoot very forcefully, or have a sensitive forefoot will require more cushioning in front. Others need only a moderate amount.

These factors are important, because there is bound to be a certain amount of trading off between different aspects of shoe design. More cushioning and support generally require a little more weight, though this can be improved with better materials and design. More cushioning inevitably requires greater thickness in the soles, if one uses the best available materials to do the job. This is because cushioning amounts to controlling the rate at which the striking foot slows down. If you allow the foot to sink twice as far before it stops, you have provided twice as much cushioning. This requires a thicker sole. Thick soles don't always provide good cushioning, but any sole that does provide it has to be relatively thick. Extra width is then often used to give the thick sole stability; otherwise you would feel as though you were running on floppy stilts. The width does not cushion your landing, but it is often necessary in designing a shoe that does.

Thickness may also be at odds with flexibility in the forefoot. Unless there are special design features that permit bending in that area, a thicker sole is less flexible, and this contributes to shinsplints and Achilles strain in some runners. The front of the shoe should be quite flexible. This is one respect in which Waffle and ripple soles have some advantage.

Support is as important for many runners as cushioning. Details on various types of feet and their needs for support are covered in Chapters Seventeen and Eighteen, and you should consider your foot type when choosing shoes. Extra support is most commonly required in the heel and along the inside edge of the foot. All good training shoes should have a solid heel counter that provides good lateral support for your heel. A flared sole does no good if none of the support is transferred to the heel of your foot. You can easily check this when you are trying shoes on. Try to turn your foot back and forth. If your heel just slops back and forth, it's not getting any support. Shoes with unstable heels are particularly bad for trail running, because they make it very easy to sprain an ankle.

Many runners have feet that roll too far inward, placing

stress on the rest of the leg (the mechanics are covered more thoroughly in Chapter Eighteen). This is the common problem usually called "flatfeet." Most people with flatfeet actually have prominent arches if they look at their feet when they are picked up. The arches seem to disappear when the person stands, because the feet roll inward. Support along the inside edges of the shoes can help prevent overuse injuries in many such people. Good shoes to check if you think you need this type of support are the Brooks Vantage Supreme and the Etonic Street Fighter. The market changes every year, but these shoes should provide a good basis for comparison. Additional heel support may be provided by an experimental rear lacing system still being tested by Etonic at the time this is being written.

Still another factor related to cushioning and stability is the heel lift, which helps to relieve pressure on the Achilles tendon. It is particularly important if you are recuperating from an Achilles injury (see Chapter Six). The lift is equal to the height of the heel minus the height of the sole at the forefoot. Clearly, if a given heel height is chosen as a maximum in the interest of stability, then more cushioning in the forefoot will result in less heel lift.

In construction the heel lift is almost always provided by the crepe wedge inserted in the sole between the tread material and the midsole. This height is easily seen from the outside of the shoe. For most runners the minimum lift should be one half-inch, and more may be desirable, particularly after an injury.

Shoe Maintenance

Most runners wear out the tread of their shoes unevenly. Much of the sole wears down very slowly, but the small areas where the sole first comes into contact with the ground and first leaves it are abraded much more quickly. This is particularly true if your foot twists as it lands or pushes off. Worn places on the soles of your shoes can significantly change the movement of your foot as it settles and pushes off during each step. The result is that overuse injuries are often caused by worn soles. Unfortunately the people who are most likely to have trouble are also the ones who wear their soles most quickly. Since not many runners can afford a new pair of shoes every week or every month, regular maintenance is necessary to keep wear in check.

Several techniques are possible. I have found two of them that work well. If a section of your sole is really worn down, it can be easily repaired by cutting a rectangular portion of the tread out with a knife or razor blade. Rip this piece off with a pair of pliers. Cut a piece the same size from an old inner tube, clean it well with alcohol, and glue it on to replace the sole material with contact cement. Once you have developed the knack, the whole procedure takes only a few minutes.

The other method is to keep the areas of the sole that wear out built up with glue. The glue that comes in tubes does not work very well for this purpose, and it takes too long to dry. The best method is to buy a hot glue gun from a hardware store. These guns use glue sticks that are melted in the gun and applied from a nozzle. They are relatively inexpensive, and the shoes are ready to use as soon as the glue has cooled. The technique is to apply a thin layer of glue to the soles as soon as you buy the shoes, on those spots that normally wear out quickly. When the glue wears off, apply another layer. Sometimes you will wear completely through the glue layer and grind a little sole away, but this is easily built back up with a new application. Never build the glued area any higher than the surrounding sole. Keep it level and even.

Regular use of a glue gun should enable you to keep a set of soles in reasonable condition until the upper of the shoes begins to fall apart.

Waffle-type treads are made from a harder material than embossed tread, and it doesn't hold glue quite as well. Fill in the area between a number of the protrusions to give the glue something to grip. It is also helpful before applying glue the first time to rough the area between the waffles with a piece of coarse sandpaper.

CHAPTER 6

Evaluating Injuries and Pain

T HE MOST DIFFICULT aspect of dealing with any injury is deciding what is wrong, and this is particularly true of many overuse injuries. From this judgment follows your decision as to how to handle the problem—whether to seek medical help, whether to modify training or stop altogether, and so on. Worst of all, the decision keeps coming up, because most running injuries take time to respond to any treatment. Each day you are likely to have doubts about previous decisions. The doctor diagnosing a possible case of appendicitis soon has an opportunity to check the accuracy of his diagnosis if he decides to operate! Both the runner and doctor usually have to feel their way when dealing with overuse injuries. You have to be calm and patient just when these are the most difficult qualities to summon up.

As indicated in earlier chapters, though, the key to diagnosing most running problems is to start with mundane and likely explanations rather than chase after strange and exotic ailments. The great majority of runners' problems will respond to quite simple treatment, if you have the good sense to apply it. And most of these problems turn out to be fairly simple to understand, *if* you ignore the dozens of unlikely possibilities and stick to the common, predictable runners' ailments. Treat shinsplints as shinsplints, and don't start worrying about compartment syndrome unless you still have the same symptoms after a couple of months of suitable training and treatment.

Most of the rest of this chapter deals with the location of trouble and type of pain. Remember, though, that the solution to most injuries lies in regular stretching and a good training schedule. At least a relaxation of hard training is required to heal most injuries, and if you keep working hard, they will get worse. If you've had new orthotics prescribed for your knee pains, give them a chance to work with reduced training before you start speed work again.

Finally, remember that most overuse injuries take time to heal. There is no cheap substitute. Give any treatment you or the doctor decide on a chance to work. Two days with new shoes or a new physician will not produce miracle cures. The longer you have put up with chronic pain, the longer it is likely to take to get rid of it. When the first signs of healing come, be gentle about adding work, or you will hurt yourself again.

Back Pains

Chronic or severe back pains should be evaluated by an orthopedist, preferably one who is both familiar with and sympathetic to runners. Both stretches (for flexibility) and exercises (for strengthening the abdomen) will help prevent many of the minor lower back pains that result mainly from fatigue. If you are experiencing back pain, however, avoid stretches and exercises that involve bending the spine backward.

Self-treatment after the onset of serious back pain is not advisable, however. The symptoms that should prompt you to see a physician are either severe pain or consistent pain after workouts or on waking the next morning.

Some back pains can be caused by foot abnormalities or by unequal leg length, but there are also a host of other causes that have nothing to do with the feet or legs, so it makes sense to see an orthopedist first for back pain. Doctors vary in their opinions on the advisability of running with certain minor spinal problems, but there are some back conditions that will definitely be aggravated by the pounding that is inevitable in running. One rather common back problem that is usually not serious but will cause occasional pain is *spondylolisthesis*, in which the vertebra just above the pelvic girdle has slipped slightly forward. If this condition is diagnosed as the cause of occasional pain and you are told to stop running, you may want to seek a second opinion. Many people who suffer from this slippage can continue to run.

Back problems are sometimes accompanied by spasm of the hamstrings or signs of *sciatica*, shooting pains running down from the lower back through the inside of the thighs and sometimes as far down as the big toe. If such shooting pains occur in connection with lower back pain, the sciatica probably originates in the back, though it can also be caused by problems in the legs. As mentioned in Chapter Four, however, sciatica is not common among runners, and many deep pains in the buttocks that are diagnosed as sciatica are actually muscle pulls.

Sciaticalike symptoms associated with back pain probably *are* sciatica, caused by irritation of the sciatic nerve, a major nerve running down from the back. Distinction of such symptoms from similar ailments when back pain is *not* present is covered later in the chapter.

Treatment Principles

Before continuing our discussion of specific parts of the body—proceeding downward from the back—we need to discuss proper treatment for some specific types of injuries. There are some important general principles that apply to most of the injuries that runners are likely to sustain. First aid is ICE—Icing, Compression, and Elevation. If you pull a muscle, sprain your ankle, or get a sore tendon, this is the first procedure to follow when you get home. Rub the area with ice or a cold pack, compress it with an elastic bandage or other wrap if the location makes this feasible, and elevate the injured limb if possible. This treatment is helpful for all injuries that come on suddenly and almost all chronic ones.

Icing is easily accomplished with cubes, with an ice bag, with a plastic bag of ice, or with commercially available cold packs that can be strapped around your leg. A convenient method for those using ice as regular therapy while an injury is healing is to put paper cups of water in the freezer and to use them for the icing. The paper can be torn back as the ice melts, so you have something to hold on to and a conveniently sized piece of ice. Styrofoam cups are even nicer for insulating your hand, though they don't break off quite so neatly. Ice an injury for twenty minutes at a time. After sustaining a painful injury you should repeat the icing about four times in the first twenty-four hours.

The reason the ICE procedure works is easily explained. Injuries always involve some physical damage to the tissues.

These may be rather massive, as in the case of a bone avulsion (where a piece of bone is ripped off) or a bad muscle strain, or they may be very tiny tears, as in the case of many overuse injuries. Bleeding or leakage of blood serum occurs at the site of the injury, causing swelling, stiffening, and

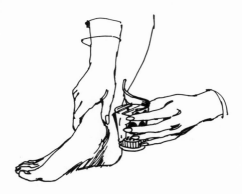

Icing is the best initial treatment for any injury involving tissue damage, because it reduces pain, bleeding within the damaged area, and swelling. Styrofoam cups filled with water and kept in the freezer provide a convenient method of icing, allowing you to comfortably grip the ice while rubbing the injured area.

pain. Healing is slowed while this swelling remains, because circulation is congested. Icing, compression, and elevation of an injured limb all reduce the amount of bleeding and swelling that occurs and thus alleviate pain. (The ice also numbs pain, of course.) Even local inflammations are often helped by this method.

At a later stage of the injury, when healing is taking place, heat may help. Heat will stimulate circulation, so it is not desirable immediately after an injury or soon after running when you are working through an injury. At these times ice is far preferable.

Muscle Pulls

A sudden muscle pull can be a minor injury or a fairly serious one. *The seriousness cannot be accurately gauged immediately after the injury occurs.* You should treat it with icing, compression, and elevation and wait twenty-four hours before trying to decide how serious it is. There's no harm in waiting a day or so before deciding whether to see a doctor, unless pain is severe or something more than a muscle seems to be involved. The physician won't be able to accurately diagnose the degree of damage until twenty-four hours have passed, either, unless the injury is serious enough to have caused a deformity because of complete muscle tissue separation. This can be ascertained by inspecting and feeling both sides of your body to see whether there are obvious differences. A hollow with a large lump below at the general site of the pain, for example, will certainly indicate that a muscle has pulled loose. This type of injury is very uncommon, particularly in distance runners. Remember also that pain around a bone should prompt you to seek medical help and X rays—this is particularly important for adolescents.

A first-degree strain involves only a few fibers of the muscle or tendon. Third-degree strain is a complete separation, and second-degree covers the wide range in between. If there is some swelling and pain after twenty-four hours, but you have full range of motion, the injury is first-degree. Second-degree strains will involve considerable swelling and pain, and motion will be limited. With a third-degree strain, it will be impossible to move the limb on its own power in the direction in which the affected muscle-tendon unit normally pulls it. When motion is seriously limited after twenty-four hours, you should see a doctor or a good trainer.

The first day after pulling a muscle, if you cannot walk without a serious limp, you should use crutches to avoid further damage. Of course, immediately after a painful misstep you will limp badly, and if this pain goes away quickly and keeps improving, you don't need to go and rent a pair of crutches. But if the pain is worse after an hour and the limb is getting stiffer, you should be icing and compressing the injury—and you should use crutches until you're sure just how serious it is.

To understand the method of treatment for strains, it is important to realize that muscle and tendon tissue do not regenerate well after being torn. The injured fibers will be rejoined by scar tissue, which is rather inelastic and tends to grow in a random, matted pattern. If this process is allowed to occur without interference, the muscle-tendon unit will heal so that it is shorter and less flexible than before. As we will see in later chapters, tightness is often the cause of pulls in the first place, so the additional tension and weakness produced by the growth of matted scar tissue will increase the likelihood of another strain. This syndrome of repeated muscle pulls in the same area has crippled many fine runners unnecessarily.

Continue periodic icing up to two days after the injury—four or five twenty-minute sessions daily. And if you can't walk without a severe limp, you should stay on crutches. But after the first forty-eight hours, when healing can be expected to have begun, it is important to begin a program of gentle stretching and moderate but progressive exercise of the muscle. The stretches should *always* be static stretches without body weight pressing on the muscle, so that the tension can be carefully controlled. The stretching principles that are detailed in Chapters Eight and Nine should be followed, but not too vigorously. The idea is to keep the scar tissue that is growing aligned with the extension of the muscle, so that the muscle does not become tighter. But force must be limited to avoid causing a new injury.

Stretching should begin with a gentle stretch of the affected muscle lasting between thirty seconds and a minute. Repeat the stretch twice more after intervals of several minutes. Do the three stretches three times daily. As the days go on, each stretch should last a little longer. Proceed slowly and cautiously. Stretching must follow on the trail of the healing process but must not interfere with it.

Exercises are also needed. The muscle will weaken from disuse; it was probably already weaker than the neighboring muscles, or it would not have been injured in the first place. And exercises promote healing if they are done gently. Exercises can be done against the resistance of someone holding your leg, against your other leg, or with weights if you have access to them. Don't overdo things or add resistance quickly. Emphasis should be on many repetitions against light resistance. One can start on quadriceps or hamstring exercises with a heavy ski boot on the foot. If you have access to a weight machine, start with no more than ten pounds and add ten more every ten days. Start with twenty repetitions three times a day. After the first two weeks, in addition to twenty repetitions with the light weight three times each day, you can do ten repetitions with twice as much weight once each day.

Palpation

Palpation means feeling parts of the body to locate pain exactly and to find abnormalities. An expert doctor can learn an amazing amount through palpation, and so can a good trainer in the limited range of athletic injuries. The amateur cannot expect to do so well, because most of us do not have a detailed knowledge of the body's structure beneath the skin. But many running injuries are simple enough that much can be learned about them from palpation.

One of the most useful tricks in examining injuries is the comparison of the injured leg or side to the uninjured one. This method can be used equally well for visual examination and palpation. You can see or feel whether an area is swollen, flushed, or deformed. You can also compare sensations—the tenderness of a tendon or a muscle to squeezing, for example. When you have doubts, squeeze the spot on both legs, or go back and forth between them. There are always some differences between limbs, but normally they are minor.

Palpation is often a good way of diagnosing a stress fracture or a tendon injury. If you can feel along a bone or pinch or squeeze along the length of a tendon and locate a single spot that is painful to palpation, you have positively identified the injury. The lack of sensitivity of one spot along a bone may not rule out a stress fracture, but the presence of a painful spot is a sure sign of a stress fracture, unless you have had a blow to the area that might have bruised the bone. Palpation can often be used to distinguish a stress fracture from irritation of a tendon sheath of a muscle pull, or to distinguish tendon injuries from irritated tendon sheaths or bursitis.

Tendon Strains

Injured tendons are among the most common running injuries, and they are also among the most frequently maltreated. Achilles injuries are especially common, and runners often keep training on them, causing further damage.

Tendons are not elastic, so if they are placed under too

much tension, they can be badly torn. Running with a torn tendon clearly presents a strong possibility of even more serious damage. Tendons have a very poor blood supply, and for this reason they heal very slowly. Tendonitis often becomes more and more acute when you keep running with it, because the tendon is far less likely than other tissues to be able to repair damage during the period from one run to the next. Its blood supply is not good enough for rapid regeneration.

Treatment for tendon strains requires *rest* combined with gentle stretching, so that the fibers of the scar tissue align themselves in the direction of the other fibers in the tendon. Most tendon strains will heal in two weeks if they are allowed to rest, and half of the remainder will heal in another week. Very few need surgery, but you will greatly increase the chance of requiring it if you try to keep running with a tendon injury. In the case of tendon strains that can be palpated, like the Achilles, the injured spot will no longer be sensitive to pressure when it is well enough to permit training.

Training after a tendon strain should begin gradually, with no speed work or hill climbing for some time. Possible causes of the strain should be corrected. Stretching and warming up should be carried out religiously.

Hip Pains

The hip is a complex area, and it is often difficult for the nonprofessional to distinguish what is going on there. Since the hip is a ball-and-socket joint, an elaborate system of muscles and tendons is required to control its motion, passing the joint at various depths. Some of these are muscles anchored on the pelvic girdle, some at the spine, and they may terminate either above or below the knee. These are the strongest muscles in the body, and the joint itself has to withstand large stresses. Around all these structures the complicated network of nerves and blood vessels serving the leg has to pass. During running, the pelvis itself has to rotate, and besides moving forward or back, the thighbone turns back and forth to provide the cushioning effect of foot pronation and to compensate for the motion of the pelvis. (See Chapters Seventeen and Eighteen for details on these movements.)

The first step in approaching hip problems is to analyze the location of the pain, including the origin if the pain has since become more generalized. The type of pain and the mode of onset are very important. Shooting, burning pains are an indication that nerves are involved. Sudden occurrence probably indicates a strain of a muscle or tendon or a bone avulsion. A pain deep in the meaty part of the buttock will be a pulled muscle or tendon, unless it is a nerve-type pain.

Muscle and tendon injuries ache and may spread over a wide area, though at the initial pull there may be a knifelike stab. Injuries involving bone avulsion, most likely in adolescents, will be deep and boring. Stress fractures, bursitis, joint inflammation, and some tendonitis and ligament problems are likely to begin slowly, getting progressively worse. Pain associated with a nerve is likely to be a burning, shocking, or shooting sort of pain.

Persistent nerve-type pains deep in the hip probably come from the sciatic nerve, especially if they shoot from the back or on down the leg. One good test is to stand or lie down and pull the affected leg up as high as you can against your abdomen, bending your knee and pointing your toe. Stretch the leg up, pulling with both hands as far as possible, but only to the point of pain. This action will stretch the sciatic nerve, and if your trouble is sciatica you will probably be rewarded with shooting pains along the path of the nerve down the inside of the thigh and on through the calf, perhaps as far as the big toe. If this test or other indications lead you to suspect sciatica, you should see a physician. Since spinal problems are the most likely cause, a general practitioner or an orthopedic specialist should probably be consulted first. But if the physician feels you have sciatica and is unable to find a cause, remember that unequal leg length and excessive foot motion sometimes cause this ailment. If orthopedic specialists cannot help, it would be worth at least consulting a podiatrist.

It is important to emphasize, however, that sciatica is uncommon among runners. *Deep pain in the fleshy part of the hip*, particularly if no back pain is present, is more likely to come from a muscle pull than from sciatica. Unequal leg length has been mentioned in many recent articles as a possible cause of sciatic pain, but it should be pointed out that self-evaluation of unequal leg length is not very easily accomplished. Even specialists have a hard time making exact leg measurements. So unless you know that you have a congenitally short leg or have had a traumatic injury in the past that might have caused one, it is best to leave this determination to the specialists.

A *generalized pain that develops slowly around the bony prominence at the lower rear hip* can be caused by bursitis. This bony projection is part of the thighbone. Along the outside of the upper leg there is a band of fibrous tissue extending all the way from the top edge of the hip down to the lower part of the knee. This band, called the *iliotibial band*, helps to stabilize the upper leg and knee during running, by preventing unwanted side-to-side motion. As the leg moves forward and back, the iliotibial band slides across the bony projection of the lower hip, and this motion sometimes irritates the bursa (fluid-filled sac) that is placed there to smooth the motion. The bursa can become inflamed, causing painful bursitis. (The technical term for this inflammation is *tro-*

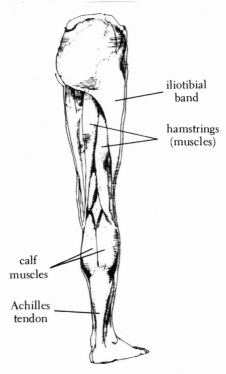

The structure of the back of the leg. There are many more muscles and tendons than shown here. The iliotibial band, *as described in the text, is a ligamentlike band that stretches over both the hip and knee joints. The* hamstrings, *which attach with tendons to both sides of the knee, and the* calf muscles *(only the outermost is shown) are the most frequently pulled in runners. The* Achilles tendon *is the second most frequently injured structure, after the knee. It extends to the bottom of the heel bone.*

chanteric bursitis, because it is an inflammation of the bursa over the greater trochanter, the projection at the top of the thighbone.)

If you suspect bursitis, lie down on the floor on your side with the painful hip up. Have someone press down against your upper foot while you raise the leg straight up to the side. Your helper should allow you to raise the leg, simply providing resistance against the movement. If you experience a lot of pain in raising the leg, your problem is a muscle strain rather than bursitis.

If the pain isn't bothersome, continue to lie on your good side, and swing the painful leg back and forth in a wide arc, as though you were running. Keep your upper hand on the painful protrusion of the hip, or have your friend do so. In many cases of bursitis, you will be able to feel the iliotibial band snapping back and forth across the bone. You have to swing your leg back and forth over the full range. If you do feel the snapping, your problem is almost certainly bursitis, but the snapping may not be apparent in mild cases.

Bursitis can be persistent and difficult to get rid of, and the farther it is allowed to progress, the more intractable it is likely to get. Ice packs and aspirin will help, but I recommend that you see a doctor if you suspect trochanteric bursitis. Bursitis is one of the very few running disorders where injection with cortisone or other steroids is justified. (Steroids have sometimes been misused in treating the chronic pains experienced by runners, and they can have very undesirable effects. You should discuss them with the doctor if such treatment is recommended. In the treatment of running injuries steroids are used mainly for bursitis and tenosynovitis—inflammation of a tendon sheath. But even for these disorders steroid treatment should not be prolonged.)

There are a number of possible causes of bursitis in the

lower hip. These include mechanical imbalances such as a short leg or a thighbone that has an abnormal angle. Early treatment by a physician who understands running injuries may save you a lot of trouble.

In an adolescent runner, a gradual onset of pain in the upper hip almost always indicates a stress fracture in the growth plate of the bone there. It requires rest and should be examined by a specialist.

Pain in the Thigh and Groin

Most of this subject has already been discussed under the general heading of muscle pulls. Stress fractures in the femur—the thighbone—are unlikely in runners.

Though the musculature in the thigh is fairly complex, this needn't really concern the runner, since treatment for a sore muscle or a strain can be applied simply enough without precise knowledge of the exact sinew involved. For mild muscle pain, icing, careful stretching, and reduced training should bring about a recovery. For a more serious pull, follow the regimen suggested earlier in the chapter.

The overall muscle group involved is of some importance, since stretching and exercise of an injury is the key to avoiding repeated injuries of the same type. Regular stretching is critical, together with exercise to regain former strength and then to bring the affected muscle group and its counterpart in the other leg to adequate strength so that future injuries are avoided. Stretches and exercises are shown in Chapters Eight to Eleven. Remember that excessively vigorous stretching, pushing too quickly to resume hard training, or adding weights too rapidly will retard healing rather than speed it.

Knee Pain

The knees are the runner's most vulnerable spots; they account for more injuries than any other area of the body. There are good reasons for this. One is that the knees act as important shock absorbers for the legs. The road shock that gets past your shoes is transmitted up through the bones. Some of it is softened by the lowering action of the feet, a mechanism that is discussed in detail in Chapters Seventeen and Eighteen. The knees absorb most of the remainder. You normally run with your knees slightly bent, and they give slightly as you hit the ground, with the shock being absorbed by the muscles at the front of the thigh and the anchor that holds them. This structure runs across the front of the knee.

Another reason for the high incidence of injuries in the knees is that they are a logical place for excessive training to take its toll. As we found in earlier chapters, the tissue around the joints responds more slowly to the stimulus of training than do the muscles, circulatory system, or the lungs. If a runner is pushing ahead too fast, it is the ligaments, tendons, and some of the other structures around the joints that are most likely to break down under the strain. And in most people the most vulnerable joint is the knee.

The knee is especially susceptible to damage because it is a hinge-type joint. The lower leg can move forward and back on the knee, but has very little side-to-side flexibility. The hip joint above is a ball-and-socket joint that has a wide range of motion in all directions. The ankle and its associated joints are more limited, but they do allow the foot to rotate in any direction within certain constraints. Both the hip and the ankle can therefore accommodate themselves to rotational stresses and forces that place much more strain on the knee. The motions of the leg and foot are discussed in more detail in Chapters Seventeen and Eighteen, together with some of the causes of various knee injuries. This section concentrates simply on identification of some of the more common problems.

It is important to emphasize throughout, however, that overtraining is once again the main culprit. The psychology of training makes us want to push hard and to look for short-cuts around the principle of the slow buildup of stress. The knees are the most frequent victims of our excessive zeal. Many weaknesses in the knees can be reduced by the use of foot supports or other remedies to improve the mechanical action of the feet and legs, but nothing will make your legs indestructible.

Heavy training is hard on the knees, and they will often not tolerate a rapid buildup. This is particularly true when you are running on pavement, which imposes additional stress on the knees both because of the shock of each step and because the regularity of the surface emphasizes any mechanical problems in the feet and legs. Twisting action is also transmitted up the legs more strongly because of the excellent grip of your soles on pavement.

One other caution should be made in dealing with knee pain in general. The discussions in this book deal only with overuse injuries of the knee. The knee is an extremely complex joint, and there are many knee problems that are not well understood even by specialists who have dealt with thousands of cases of knee damage. This book will not make you into a qualified orthopedic surgeon. If you have had traumatic injuries to your knees from skiing, football, or other activities, running may cause your old ailments to flare up. For many runners, slow, careful training will strengthen these old wounds, but if you have persistent pain, you should either slack off or see a specialist.

There are also many new problems that can occur to people who have no history of injury. If you have any sudden and severe pains in your knees, see a doctor, and if you have chronic difficulties, use your common sense. If the remedies you try don't work, or if you can make no sense of your troubles, see a doctor who is sympathetic to running. Above all, don't persist pigheadedly in some training schedule regardless of knee pains. I know of people who will probably never be able to run long distances because they have injured their knees so badly by holding to rigid training schedules and running long races in spite of knee pain.

Generalized knee pain is usually the result of overtraining. You can't ignore knee pain just because you feel good elsewhere. Your knees are sending you a message: Slow down! Badly chosen or poorly maintained shoes are another frequent cause of knee troubles. (See the notes in the preceding chapter.) If you have the same trouble regardless of apparently good shoes, no matter how slowly you increase your work load, foot imbalances may be the cause of your difficulties. Study the discussion in Chapter Eighteen, or see a podiatrist to have your feet checked.

Pain on the outer side of the knee can be caused by tendon or ligament damage and should be palpated to find any sensitive spots. Often, however, there is a generalized pain, tenderness, and swelling that indicate bursitis. Like bursitis in the lower hip, inflammation of the bursa on the outside of the knee results from the movement under pressure of the iliotibial band, that strong group of fibrous tissue connecting the upper edge of the hip with the leg below the knee. Treatment should include aspirin, which is antiinflammatory, and hot towels for twenty minutes four times daily, with a complete rest from running for six weeks if the knee has become very painful. I suggest, though, that if you suspect bursitis, you see a physician familiar with running injuries. Bursitis needs to be treated early, because it can become stubborn if it is left to get worse. Steroids may help, and they should certainly be tried in a persistent case before resorting to surgery.

Bursitis on the outside of the knee and other pains there

can be caused by worn shoes, by high-arched, inflexible feet, by running on the sloping sides of roads with pronounced crowns in the center or around small tracks in the same direction (injury to the outside knee—the one farther from the center of the road). For all these causes and the appropriate corrective measures, see Chapter Eighteen.

Pain on the inner side of the knee is more common than on the outside. This is probably true for two reasons. The ligaments on the outside are stronger, resisting deformation more effectively. The foot defects likely to cause pain on the inside of the knee are also more common than those usually associated with pains on the outside. Note that inside knee pain is often associated with pain around the kneecap (see below).

Injuries on the inside of the knee are most commonly a result of tendon strain, and they should be treated that way initially, as long as they are relatively mild and seem to respond to treatment. Icing, compression, and elevation should help, together with reduced mileage or a temporary change to another form of exercise if pain is worsened by easy running. Immediate attention should be paid to the cause of the injury. Possible causes include poorly chosen or badly worn shoes, feet that pronate excessively, and running on crowned roads or around small tracks in the same direction (injury to the inside knee—the one *closer* to the center of the road). See Chapter Eighteen for causes and corrective measures.

Pain around the kneecap can be caused by problems in the joint, by tendonitis, or by ligament damage. In runners it is most commonly caused by irritation of the back of the kneecap as it rubs up and down on the bony groove of the thigh bone. The mechanism of this injury is discussed in detail in Chapter Seventeen. Typical symptoms of this problem (*chondromalacia of the patella*—softening of the cartilage on the back of the kneecap) are pain after sitting for some time, pain associated with climbing up and down stairs, pain on squatting, and grinding sounds in the knees. Chondromalacia often occurs in both knees, though perhaps with different degrees of severity.

To check for chondromalacia, sit on the edge of a chair with both legs sticking straight out, heels on the floor and knees straight. Adjust your position so that your legs are straight but the muscles are relaxed. Grasp the kneecap of the affected knee with a thumb and forefinger so that you can hold it and press down. Now tighten the muscles in the front of your thigh. They will pull the kneecap up. Slowly allow the kneecap to move, continuing to resist the movement somewhat and pressing down. If you have chondromalacia you will feel a good deal of pain as the kneecap turns and rides up, and there is likely to be grinding as well. If you don't feel pain at the back of your kneecap, your problem is elsewhere.

Treatment for chondromalacia is icing after running. A knee brace during and after running is often helpful, primarily to provide compression and prevent swelling, though the brace may also stabilize the kneecap somewhat. Aspirin may help. Quadriceps exercises are very important; begin them immediately (see Chapter Eleven).

The root causes of chondromalacia are the same ones listed above in connection with pain on the inner side of the knee, and chondromalacia is often associated with some irritation of the tendons there. Correction of mechanical imbalances that may be causing the problem is essential to pain-free running and is discussed in detail in Chapters Seventeen and Eighteen. Chondromalacia in runners is usually a result of imbalances in the feet, so some kind of additional support is necessary.

It should be noted that some physicians distinguish chondromalacia from *runner's knee,* considering the latter to be a milder irritation of the back of the kneecap that precedes softening of the cartilage. Diagnosis and treatment are the same—the difference lies only in the severity of the problem.

Pain behind the knee results from irritation of the tendons of the hamstrings or the calf muscles, almost always due to overtraining. It is a relatively common injury in beginners. Icing, reduced training, and religiously practiced stretching routines should effect a cure.

Pain in the Lower Leg

Pain in the meaty part of the calf is nearly always an indication of muscle strain. It should be treated with ice, compression, stretching, and either reduced training or rest, depending on the severity of the strain. If there is real pain and not just a simple ache, you should switch to another form of exercise until the muscle has recovered. (See Chapter Twelve.) Pains in the tendonous area farther down are discussed below.

Aching pain deep in the calf can result from either a stress fracture in one of the lower leg bones or from muscle strain in the *posterior tibial muscle,* the muscle that runs behind the larger bone of the lower leg. These ailments are most conveniently considered along with shinsplints.

Shinsplints and other aching pains in the front of the lower leg are the curse of many athletes returning to training, of beginners, and of some runners who are unusually vulnerable to this injury. These nagging pains, common as they are, are often misunderstood. Shinsplints will be discussed first, because they are far more widespread than some of the other ailments with similar symptoms. Shinsplints are overuse injuries of the muscles and tendons of the front part of the leg. They are not terribly serious injuries, but severe cases can be disabling and persistent, so they are no joking matter.

The muscles at the front of the lower leg are used to lift

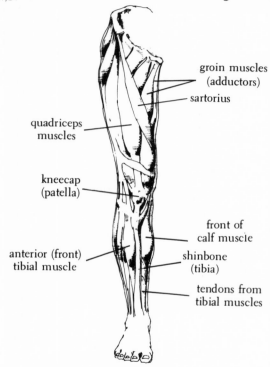

groin muscles
(adductors)

sartorius

quadriceps
muscles

kneecap
(patella)

front of
calf muscle

anterior (front)
tibial muscle

shinbone
(tibia)

tendons from
tibial muscles

The structure of the front of the leg. The quadriceps *(meaning four muscles, all attaching to the kneecap) make up the bulk of the muscle mass at the front of the thigh. They are bound by a tendon to the* kneecap, *which is in turn attached by ligaments to the* shinbone *or* tibia. *More detail on the knee is shown in Chapter Seventeen. The* sartorius *is most frequently a source of injury in adolescents. The tibia or shinbone is the main bone of the lower leg.*

the foot upward. Pull your toes and the ball of your foot up as hard as you can, and you will feel these muscles harden and tighten. Like the quadriceps in the front of the thigh, these muscles are generally much weaker in distance runners than the more powerful calf muscles behind, and this is one reason why they're vulnerable to overuse injuries, especially after a layoff that has allowed them to weaken more. It stands to reason that strengthening and stretching exercises for these muscles are among the best preventive measures against shinsplints.

One of the common causes of shinsplints is running on harder surfaces than your legs are used to. When you do this, there is a greater shock each time your heel hits the ground. To protect yourself from the impact, you instinctively raise your toes up high and then let your foot drop down gradually, absorbing the shock along the way. The muscles that are letting your foot down are the muscles in the front of the leg, and the unfamiliar stress is likely to leave them sore and mildly injured. For the same reasons, many changes in training routine or in shoes can precipitate a case of shinsplints.

(The shin is the sharp crest you feel along the front of your lower leg. The name of the bone is the *tibia*. It is the main weight-bearing bone of the lower leg, and the inner of the two bones of the lower leg. Its top is a double socket that forms the bottom half of the knee joint, and its bottom is the bump on the inside of the ankle. There are two primary muscles associated with it, and shinsplints are the result of overuse damage to these muscles or their tendons. The fleshy area you can feel on the outside front of your lower leg, a little way below the knee, is the *anterior tibial muscle,* which simply means the front tibial muscle. The other is deep in the leg behind the tibia and is called the *posterior tibial muscle.*)

These muscles also connect in a complicated way to the arch of the foot and help support it. Because of this, runners with weak arches or other foot defects or with poorly chosen shoes may have a lot of trouble with shinsplints. Correction for these mechanical difficulties is discussed in Chapter Eighteen. Runners whose shinsplints result primarily from mechanical problems must have suitable foot supports if other treatment for shinsplints is to be effective.

Treatment for shinsplints consists of icing, compression, elevation, and reduction of training. Shoes with good cushioning and firm support should be used if you continue running; and if soft surfaces are available, running on them may be a help. Avoid overstriding, since the foot then hits hard on the heel and has to be lowered by the tibial muscles. It is often helpful to try to run "softly," landing on the feet with as little impact as possible. Rest from training may be required to allow the muscles to heal themselves, and running may have to be replaced by another activity for a while. Pain should be your guide. Once shinsplints have been suffered, several days to a few weeks of rest or easy running will be necessary before you run seriously again. At the very least you should greatly reduce your mileage and avoid speed work or hills until the pain has disappeared.

One other cause of shinsplints should be mentioned, because it strikes many experienced runners unexpectedly and may not be suspected as the source of trouble. Running on slippery surfaces such as hard snow, ice, or slick mud can cause pronounced shinsplints. Running style is radically changed to cope with the poor footing, and this change puts unaccustomed stress on the anterior tibial muscle. I believe the reason is that the whole foot is pulled up at the end of the stride with the forefoot held high instead of toeing off as usual. A powerful push-off would make your foot slip. This change in stride can result in a strained muscle. The problem is not serious, but it's mentioned here so that runners who experience it will not suspect stress fractures or other more obscure ailments.

Stress fractures can also cause pain in the lower leg, and it may be difficult to tell them from shinsplints. In general, however, it is safe to assume that shinsplints are the cause. They are far more common than stress fractures. Palpate the shinbone to be sure that one tender spot cannot be located, which would indicate a stress fracture. Deep, boring pain should also make you suspicious. Shinsplints tend to ache and often affect both the muscle body and the tendons lower down running through the ankle and connecting it to the foot. Soreness all along the bone is usually due to small ruptures in the connections of the muscle to the bone, rather than to a stress fracture.

One other possible cause of pain in the muscles of the lower leg, also far less common than shinsplints, is *compartment syndrome*, a swelling within the muscle sheath that prevents proper return of the blood through the veins. If any of the muscle areas of the lower leg feel painful, hard, distended, and stiff, you might suspect compartment syndrome. If this condition occurs, medical attention should be sought, but this sort of acute problem is not likely. Compare the muscle area with the one on the other leg if you suspect a problem. A few individuals who have otherwise unexplained chronic shinsplints may suffer from compartment syndrome due to a tight muscle envelope. This diagnosis should be made by a physician. Remember, however, to explore the obvious explanation first.

Heel Pain

Most of the propulsive force the runner uses to drive the

body forward is transmitted to the foot through the Achilles tendon, which attaches the calf muscles to the heel bone. This tendon withstands a great deal of stress at every step the runner takes. It wraps around most of the back side of the heel bone, attaching at the lower rear. This gives the calf muscles good mechanical advantage, but also increases the possibility of irritating rubbing of the tendon during the repeated actions of running. A bursa is placed between the bone and the tendon to reduce the friction.

The most common pains in the heel are due either to irritation or tearing of the Achilles tendon. Usually when there is tearing of the tendon, it can be palpated by squeezing with thumb and forefinger up and down the tendon. Any sensitivity will indicate sure damage to the tendon at that point and will rule out other possible causes of the pain. If such a spot is found, follow the treatment suggested earlier in this chapter: icing, compression, and *rest*. Two weeks of rest are usually required, and gentle stretching after a few days. If a tendon tear is found, *don't try to run through it!* You will simply make the injury worse and delay healing.

If walking is uncomfortable, a heel lift inside the shoe or built into the heel will help. The same lift should be used in the other shoe to avoid distorting the gait. A heel lift may also be helpful when training starts again, at least until stretching has reduced tension on the Achilles. Felt inserts can be used in the shoes and so can commercial heel lifts, but beware the pressure on the heel that can result from raising the heel inside the shoe. It may be better to change to a pair of shoes with higher heel wedges in the sole or to have a shoemaker install higher crepe wedges.

Good shoes and stretching are critical when you are recuperating from an Achilles injury. Once a tendon is injured, it will be more vulnerable to future damage because of the scar tissue that has grown in. Return to training slowly, with extensive stretching and warming up, and avoid hill and speed work for a while. The cause of the tendon strain can be badly chosen or poorly maintained shoes, especially unstable ones with low heels. Foot abnormalities can contribute (this is discussed in Chapters Seventeen and Eighteen), though they are more likely to be secondary factors in strains of the Achilles, while in knee injuries the feet are often the primary cause.

Generalized pain in the heel that cannot be isolated to a specific part of the tendon can be caused by stress fractures, bursitis, or irritation of the tendon sheath. Stress fractures cause a deeper pain and aching extending into the heel, and they are likely to become worse with running. Bursitis results in pain a little below the surface, where the tendon spreads over the heel. If it is not accompanied by tendonitis (and it may be), bursitis will be painful if you try to raise up on your toes and bounce, but a little stretching and warming up will allow you to do this with a minimum of pain. Tendon injuries will remain painful if you try to bounce on your toes, regardless of warm-up. Both tendonitis and bursitis are likely to bother you in the morning when you get up and at the start of a run, but they will get better as you warm up.

Bursitis can be caused by irritating rubbing of the Achilles over the heel. This friction can result from overtraining, hill work, bad shoes, or a problem with foot mechanics. Bursitis can also be caused by tight shoe heels over a period of several weeks. Treatment is to eliminate the irritant, stretch and warm up thoroughly, and ice the area after running. A persistent case may need attention from a physician and perhaps steroid injections.

Heel bumps have already been discussed thoroughly in Chapter Four. They usually begin with bursitis and general irritation around the heel. A fibrous and then bony bump forms at the site, and this soon produces irritation of the tendon and sheath, if they were not already present. Clearly, the sooner this chain is broken, the better.

Pain in the Ankle

Except for sprains (which are covered separately in Chapter Fourteen) pains in the ankle are not particularly common in runners. The joint and its surroundings are not nearly as vulnerable to overuse injuries as the knees are. *Pain developing slowly on either side of the ankle* is usually due to tendonitis, and it should be treated as such. If it is not traceable to overtraining or to poor shoes, this tendon strain is almost always attributable to mechanical problems in the foot (discussed in Chapters Seventeen and Eighteen). If you cannot solve these yourself, you should see a podiatrist.

Pain deep in the ankle that is persistent and aching even after a few days of rest is probably due to a stress fracture in one of the bones of the rear foot or ankle. It may also be the result of joint or nerve problems. Structural problems in the feet may be a precipitating cause, but once such an injury occurs, you should see a physician, preferably a sports podiatrist.

Radiating pain or numbness originating at the inside of the ankle and affecting the arch area or inside edge of the foot can be due to compression of the nerves passing into the foot, the so-called *tarsal-tunnel syndrome*. It is not common in runners, but if you have these symptoms and they persist, you should consult a physician.

Pain in the tendons running down to the arch through the ankle is a form of shinsplints, and muscle strain can usually be felt in the muscles around the tibia as well.

Pain in the Bottom of the Foot

Problems in the surface tissue of the feet have already been discussed in Chapter Three. It is important to treat difficulties like bunions and corns before they become serious. If self-treatment is unsuccessful, see a podiatrist. Remember that people vary widely in the amount of cushioning tissue on the bottoms of their feet and in their feet's sensitivity to bruising and blistering. Remember also that large calluses and bunions are due to unnatural pressure, either from poor shoes or from mechanical problems in the feet.

Pain at the bottom front of the heel or the side front of the heel, as mentioned briefly in Chapter Four, is usually due to

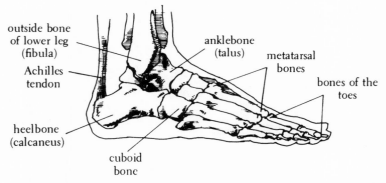

The structure of the foot, shown from the outside. The large ends of the two bones of the lower leg, the tibia *and the* fibula, *ride on either side of the* anklebone, *or talus, like a rider astride a horse. The large forces that are borne by the* Achilles tendon *are obvious from the structure.*

inflammation of the plantar fascia—the strong bands of tissue running along the bottom of the foot between the toes and the front of the heel bone. These tissues can be stressed if the foot pronates excessively (see Chapter Eighteen), if you are overtraining, if you have begun hill climbing, or if you have poor support from your shoes.

Intermittent strain-type pain in the arch area is also due to strain of the plantar fascia. Allowing this condition to become chronic can result in a nasty heel spur, bursitis, or more severe inflammation and trauma to the fascia themselves. Arch supports are needed as an essential part of treatment. Minor pains, if caught in time, may require only supports and relaxation of training. If the pain is severe, you will have to switch to another form of exercise for at least a month. The longer you let this pain go on, the harder it will be to get rid of.

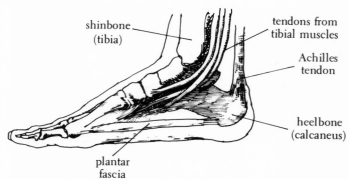

The structure of the foot as seen from the inside. The shinbone or tibia forms the bony bump on this side of the ankle. Note that the tendons from the muscles on either side of the tibia come down behind this protrusion and help to support the arch. The arch also receives support from the bowstringlike plantar fascia. Any collapsing of the arch can thus cause irritation of the plantar fascia, the front edge of the heelbone to which they connect, and to the shin muscles and tendons.

Pain in the Forefoot

Pain along the top of the forefoot can be caused either by tendonitis or by a stress fracture in one of the metatarsal bones, the long bones leading along the top of the foot to the toes. The two injuries should be distinguishable by palpation and by the type of pain. Tendonitis along the top of the foot is often caused by shoes that press too tightly there. Over a period of time they will irritate the tendons or their sheaths. The remedy is to remove the irritation, and the treatment is icing. Stress fractures, if they are not caused by a bad misstep, are likely to result from a weak, unsupported foot, perhaps combined with overtraining. (See Chapter Eighteen for correction.)

Nerve-type pain or numbness running along the bottom of the foot or between the metatarsals is due to pinched or trapped nerves. If this problem persists, it should be checked by a podiatrist.

CHAPTER 7

Finding Medical Help

THE FIELD of sports medicine has undergone a revolution during the last few years, particularly in those areas that most concern runners. Changes have occurred both in the attitudes of physicians and in the knowledge of techniques for preventing and treating certain kinds of injuries. Things are changing so fast that it is difficult to reflect current attitudes and knowledge in a book like this. Statements become outdated almost as soon as they are written.

All this ferment is of tremendous benefit to the runner because of the improvements in understanding of overuse injuries. But it can be confusing as well, since the attitude of individual doctors and their knowledge about running injuries vary so widely. There are also major disagreements both over the causes of some ailments and over the best regimen for treatment. In a field that is changing as rapidly as this one, there are few definitive answers. Each trainer or doctor has to rely on his or her own experience and that of colleagues who have shared theirs. On top of this confusion is superimposed a considerable overlay of professional rivalry and misunderstanding.

Much of the new attitude and many of the new techniques of treatment of runners' ailments have come from the field of podiatry—foot medicine. This is true partly because so many running injuries work up from the feet to the rest of the body and partly because the podiatrists jumped into the void left by a lot of other professionals, who were not very interested in looking seriously at the overuse injuries suffered by runners. All this happened at a time when the number of runners in the country was multiplying to hundreds of times what it had been before.

What the podiatrists discovered was that a large percentage of the injuries suffered by runners and by some other athletes could be successfully treated simply by providing proper supports for the feet.

The word spread like wildfire around the running community. Not only was there a group of doctors that was actually interested in trying to help runners, but they were having success with a lot of injuries that no one had been able to do much about before. Furthermore, they were often working these miracles without surgery, without demanding long layoffs from running, and relatively cheaply. Runners had not had much reason for faith in the medical profession before, for reasons ranging from incompetent diagnoses of nonexistent heart disease to surgery that was both unnecessary and unsuccessful. The growth of sports podiatry was a boon to thousands of runners who had long-standing injuries that were cured by the new miracle workers.

The attitude of much of the rest of the medical profession was also changing. Quite a few cardiologists were discovering the advantage of running programs for both the rehabilitation and prevention of cardiovascular disease. Like everyone else, a lot of doctors were starting to run, and they were as enthusiastic as other runners about the benefits of the sport. Their experiences with both the healthful effects of running and the treatment of running injuries filtered back into the medical profession. The expertise of the small group of competent sports physicians who had been around all along—many of them orthopedic specialists—began to receive more attention.

The current situation of the runner needing medical help is an odd one. There is a good deal of sniping back and forth between orthopedic specialists and podiatrists over who should be the primary physicians for runners. A lot of the barbs are justified. Orthopedic surgeons have often been a lot more interested in glamorous surgical procedures than in mundane problems like tendonitis caused by feet that roll over too far. Podiatrists, naturally enthusiastic about their discoveries and about the crowds of runners beating a path to their doors, have sometimes prescribed orthotic foot supports as the remedy for everything from hangnails to bad breath, and their estimations of the likelihood of successful treatment have often been overoptimistic. Furthermore, despite a sympathetic attitude, many podiatrists don't understand running any more than a lot of general practitioners of the past did, and their advice has sometimes reflected this lack of knowledge. As with every other specialty, there are brilliant diagnosticians in podiatry and others who are not quite so talented.

Who Can Help

For a runner who needs medical help in dealing with a debilitating injury this situation can be extremely confusing. The best strategy to follow depends on where you live and on your own particular situation. As a general rule, however, it is probably best to try to find a doctor who knows a lot about running as a first step, rather than search for a specialist in feet, knees, or backs. A doctor who is a runner or who has treated a lot of runners is probably more likely to understand runner's knee than someone who has operated on a lot of knees but knows nothing about running and cares less. Even if your running doctor is a pediatrician or a gynecologist, he'll probably be able to advise you on who to see. Don't neglect paramedical personnel if they are available. A good trainer who has worked with a lot of running injuries will know more than all but a tiny percentage of the doctors in the country about them. A competent trainer also knows his limitations and probably is familiar with all the specialists in sports medicine around the area. If you live near a large college or university, it wouldn't hurt to call up the athletic department and try to talk with the trainer responsible for the track team. The doctors for professional sports teams might also be good sources of information on local physicians, even if they are not available themselves.

Any runners you know in your area are obvious possibilities for information on local physicians. Serious racers are often particularly good sources of names and comments. They talk to other competitors, often get hurt a lot, and are likely to try any possible solution to get back to their training.

If you hear good things about one doctor from several runners who have been patients, this is the best possible recommendation.

Another possibility is to call the local medical society to ask whether there are any doctors with a particular interest in running. The same approach can be tried with hospitals. Running doctors are likely to have a reputation among their colleagues—"You know the crazy one who goes out running in the heat of the day."

Several of the preceding chapters have made specific recommendations on the type of specialist most appropriate to certain injuries. These specialists are usually listed under separate headings in the phone book. In a metropolitan area general practitioners and orthopedic specialists will be listed under *Physicians & Surgeons, (M.D.)*, usually with their specialties. Foot specialists are listed under *Podiatrists*. In either case you can call and ask whether the doctor is interested in treating runners' injuries or knows someone who is. You might get a few huffy replies, but you'll probably get the information you need as well. Podiatrists are likely to be more cooperative, because of their current interest in runners. And if you have a problem that does not seem suited to a podiatrist, you might still be able to get a recommendation of an M.D. from a podiatrist who works with runners.

The National Joggers Association, 1910 K Street, NW 202, Washington, D.C. 20006, publishes a list of podiatrists interested in running injuries. Local running clubs are also likely to know of podiatrists and other doctors interested in running. Those who have given talks at runners' clinics are always a good possibility.

Podiatrists

Despite a tendency to occasionally overemphasize the role

of the foot in running injuries, the sports podiatrist is the runner's best friend. After improper training techniques, the mechanically imbalanced foot is the greatest single cause of running injuries. Podiatrists have also been alert to related problems that often cause overuse-type injuries overlooked by other specialists, such as legs of unequal length. For most running injuries below the back, a podiatrist is probably the specialist most likely to be able to help you, particularly if he's shown an interest in runners' problems.

Part II

STRETCHES AND EXERCISES

Chapter 8

Stretching Fundamentals

WHEN IT is done properly, stretching is one of the most useful of all tools for preventing injuries and facilitating the cure of those you have already sustained. Stretching is also beautifully complementary to running for general body conditioning, because it improves your overall fitness in ways in which running itself is deficient. Besides being in poor cardiopulmonary condition, most adult Americans are dreadfully inflexible. Our daily lives are designed not only to allow us to studiously avoid exercise, but to insure that we don't very often have to bend, squat, or otherwise extend our bodies to the limits of their range of motion. We even sit on chairs so that we don't have to bend or stretch much in order to eat or relax. As a consequence, our bodies gradually become less and less lithe and supple.

Stretching is the way to reverse this stiffening process, just as running improves the condition of your breathing, circulation, endurance, and the muscle tone in your legs. One disadvantage of running is that it tends to tighten the muscles in the backs of the legs, which are already quite inflexible in most adult Americans.

Many of the overuse injuries to which runners are prone can be precipitated or aggravated by tight muscles. This is easily understood. Consider Achilles tendonitis, for example, one of the most common of runners' troubles. The Achilles pulls up on the heel and thrusts the body forward with each toe-off, withstanding quite large forces. It may also be stressed by various imbalances in the foot or by poorly chosen shoes. When tendonitis occurs, the tendon has been pulled beyond its limits and has begun to tear apart, with at least some of the fibers being damaged.

If the muscles of the calf and the tendon itself are very tight, the tendon will have to undergo additional stress at every step. The force of the body's forward motion will reach the tendon much sooner, because the foot will not be able to flex fully before the toe-off begins. When you are running hills, if the muscles and tendons at the back of the calf are flexible, you can run up rather steep grades with your foot flattening normally against the ground, thus reducing the strain on the calf and the Achilles. If these muscles and tendons are tight, you will be forced up onto your toes by a very mild grade, putting constant stress on the tendons. Obviously, if your Achilles is already being stressed near its limit, these additional burdens caused by tightness will be enough to cause an injury.

The same sort of mechanisms operate in most of the muscles of the legs and feet. Tight, inflexible muscles, tendons, and joints are far more subject to injury than those conditioned to a full range of motion.

Stretching is also extremely useful during the healing stage of many injuries, provided that it's done gently and carefully. Fibrous and inelastic scar tissue will form, and if it is permitted to grow with the muscle or tendon involved undergoing only limited motion, the elasticity after healing will be less than before. If tightness contributed to the original injury, the athlete will be reentering his sport even tighter than before and very vulnerable to reinjuring the same muscle or tendon. There are important exceptions; but in general, once healing is underway, it is important to do gentle but thorough stretching, so that the growing scar tissue is aligned in the direction in which the muscle or tendon extends, and so that it does not shorten the range of motion.

Thus stretching should be a constant tool for the runner: for general health, for preventing injuries, and for improving healing when an injury has occurred. It is not a panacea, and it won't solve all problems. If causes other than inflexibility are the root of a particular difficulty, stretching may have no beneficial effect at all. In rare cases it may exacerbate irritation that begins with another source, such as a trapped nerve or a tendon rubbing against a bone.

But it's surprising how many difficulties are improved by stretching, and how rarely it causes difficulties when it is done properly. When an overuse symptom results from a different cause, the improved flexibility that results from stretching will often still give a muscle or tendon enough additional resilience to be able to heal. Most difficulties experienced with stretching result from doing it incorrectly.

Calisthenics and Slow Stretching

In the U.S. the exercises that have been taught to improve flexibility have traditionally been of the calisthenic variety, with bouncing stretches. While these are fine for developing muscle tone and endurance, they are poor for improvement of pliability. Toe touching is the classic example. You were probably taught to bounce down rapidly and repeatedly toward your toes. Any activity of this type is better than none if it isn't overdone. But any bouncing action induces an automatic reflexive contraction in the muscles. This is a natural protective reaction to prevent the muscle from being overstretched in a vigorous activity. As a result you never reach full extension in a bouncing stretch, and it rarely improves your flexibility very much.

The proper way to stretch is to extend the muscles to their limits *slowly*, going to the limit of comfort, and then to hold the position and concentrate on relaxing the muscles being stretched. After a little while—from ten seconds to a minute—the muscle can usually be extended farther without pain or damage. The key is to hold a relaxed and comfortable stretch, not to try to bounce or force additional extension.

Bouncing not only fails to increase the flexibility of the muscles, it can cause harm if it is too vigorous. This is particularly true if you are stretching because you have already sustained some injury. Additional extension obtained by bouncing is dangerous. In general, extra range achieved by slow and controlled stretching is safe. Exceptional care is necessary only when you are stretching an injured muscle-tendon group, when you are doing a stretch where a lot of force is achieved through leverage or body weight (as with the plough, for example), or where a joint like the knee is receiving a good deal of stress. Even in these cases, working slowly and carefully will always avoid any danger.

Slow extension of the muscles and tendons will gradually make you more limber. Devoting adequate time to each stretch is important, because additional flexibility is achieved during the later phase of a stretch.

It may be worth pointing out here that most of the techniques we currently use for stretching have been adapted and simplified from the Indian discipline of yoga, more specifically from *hatha* yoga. Yoga teaches far more than stretching, and no attempt will be made in this book to explain even the physical discipline involved. Those interested in further pursuing either stretching or the full teaching of yoga should consult a yoga teacher or a book—the best of which is B.K. Iyengar's *Light on Yoga* (New York: Schocken, 1966).

Stretching Technique

There are several basic rules that apply to all stretching. You should get into the appropriate starting position first, and be sure you are oriented correctly. Breathe evenly, and concentrate on relaxing as you stretch out the muscles as far as you comfortably can. There is usually a tendency to tense up and often to hold your breath as you start to really apply tension to the muscles. Relaxation is the key to effective stretching. It is often quite difficult to relax the muscle being stretched, but it can be managed with some concentration. Proper tension is achieved when you feel the muscle stretching in a pronounced way.

Stretching should not hurt. If you feel any pain, back off. The only exception is when you are stretching an injured muscle or tendon, and this must be done very gingerly. Even then there should be very little pain. Pain is a warning sign from the body, and it should be heeded. If you have torn a tendon, you should probably be stretching in consultation with a physician. Stretching has to be very mild at first when a tendon or a bad muscle tear is healing, and it must progress *with* healing, not ahead of it.

In normal circumstances, the method is to hold the stretch, concentrating on breathing and relaxation, until you feel the muscle loosen. Then stretch slowly until you feel a good stretch again, and hold for another period of thirty seconds to a couple of minutes.

Though stretching is quite a safe activity, compulsive individuals can overdo it. Like running, stretching is a powerful tool for molding the body, and it can be misused. You cannot force flexibility on your body. It will take time to improve. There will be daily fluctuations in your ability to stretch, and there are wide variations in individual capacities.

Stretching should be a pleasant activity, intended to make you feel better, not an area in which you force yourself toward ill-conceived goals. Attempting to achieve some particular position, especially within a short time, is dangerous and foolhardy. Trying to force things in stretching is a sure way to hurt yourself. When it is properly done, stretching feels good. If you find yourself getting stiff or sore, you are on the wrong track. Relax and enjoy yourself.

Stretching Opposing Muscle Groups

People's needs and routines vary, and so will their stretching routines. If you have had trouble with your Achilles tendons, for example, you will probably want to stretch them frequently, often when you are not doing any other stretches. As a general rule, however, I think it is a good idea to stretch opposing muscle groups sequentially. I do a stretch that extends the spine backward after doing one that bends it forward. I stretch my quadriceps (the muscles at the front of the thigh) after doing hamstring stretches. (The hamstrings are the muscles at the back of the thigh.)

One does not have to be rigid about this principle, but it is important to recognize the relationship between opposing muscle groups both in flexibility and strength. Imbalances in either strength or flexibility can cause injuries, and by keeping to a pattern of this type you will remind yourself of the importance of balance.

It is just as important to maintain equilibrium between muscles on the two sides of the body. We tend to favor the side that is more flexible when we stretch, just as we use one hand to do most manual tasks. This is a mistake when it comes to stretching, particularly for the runner. A distance runner has to use both legs and both arms equally. Stretching and exercises should be directed toward equalizing the two sides of the body. There has been good statistical correlation between people who pull their hamstrings and those who have one leg that is stronger than the other. Similar correlations probably exist between flexibility differences and certain injuries.

Each stretch that does not affect the two sides of the body equally should be done on both sides. Usually it is best to stretch the less flexible side first. Most of us tend to hold the first stretch of a pair longer than the second. If there is a large difference between the two sides, it is a good idea to repeat the stretch for the tight side. For the same reasons, it is always a good idea to organize your stretching routine to start with your stiffest areas, so that you will give them the most attention.

Chapter 9

Basic Stretching Routines

U NLESS YOU are recovering from an injury or have some other special reason, it is not essential that stretching be done in immediate conjunction with your run. Many runners have developed the habit of stretching before and after running, and this is an excellent procedure. Stretching before a run is a good ingredient of your warm-up, and it helps prevent muscle pulls. Stretching after a run helps to counteract the tendency of the muscles to tighten up, especially following a hard workout. But unless you are feeling unusually tight or are trying to loosen up for a hard training session or a race, it does not seem to be too important whether stretching is done at the same time of day as your running or worked in elsewhere. If you run at a period in the day when your time is limited, it may be much more sensible to stretch at another time.

The important thing is to make stretching a regular habit, like your running. Associate it with particular occasions, so that you stretch thoroughly every day. Like other resolutions, the one to stretch is easily dropped, unless it is made a part of one's daily routine. This is easier to do with stretching than with running itself, because stretching is so easy to do. You don't have to map out a time block if it is more convenient for you to work different stretches in at odd intervals during the day. Stretches can become useful devices for relaxing your body or your mind.

Though spreading your stretching routine through the day may make it easier to skip at first, it does have the advantage of ensuring that you will do a thorough job as a matter of course once the habit is firmly established. You can do Achilles stretches just as well while you are waiting for the bus or reading a report as at any other time of day.

Always stretch before, after, and sometimes during a run if you are feeling unusually tight, if you are working through an injury, or if you are doing a hard workout early in the day, when the muscles have not had time to limber up. This type of stretching routine does not have to be complete. Rather than do all your stretches, you can concentrate on the few muscles that need stretching. Before an early morning run, for example, I always do stretches for the calves, hamstrings, and the muscles at the front of the legs, but I usually leave other stretches until later in the day.

Groups of Stretches

Any good yoga or stretching book will illustrate hundreds of different stretches, most of which are useful. The ones illustrated here concentrate on those areas that commonly trouble runners. If you have problems with tightness in a particular part of your body, experiment with stretching techniques that may alleviate the inflexibility. The stretches here are classified in groups according to the muscles that they stretch. The emphasis for runners, of course, is on the legs, and secondarily on the back, which has to be supple and strong enough to carry the upper body easily. Most stretches, particularly those derived from yoga, actually stretch several muscle groups, but the influence on the leg muscles is what most concerns us.

The illustrations do not show the ideal poses that can be found in yoga texts. They are drawn to show the range that typically tight runners are likely to reach after stretching for a little while. You will probably find some stretches to be easier and some harder. Remember that the important goal is to get a good stretch in the appropriate muscle group and to hold and then extend the stretch. Whether you can bend only half as far as shown in the drawing or you can do much better is not particularly important. You should achieve a good stretch without straining.

In some cases only one stretch for a particular muscle group is shown, while in others there are two or three. Runners should normally include at least one stretch from each group in their routines, or an appropriate substitute. If toe touching is a good hamstring stretch for you, it can easily be substituted for the ones shown here, for example.

STRETCHES FOR THE CALF MUSCLES AND THE ACHILLES TENDONS

This is the standard stretch for the Achilles, and it works well. Make sure your rear heel touches the floor and that your back leg is straight. Shift your rear foot into several positions so that the whole back of the leg is stretched. Work on only one leg at a time.

An even better stretch for the Achilles tendons and the calves uses any adjustable inclined surface. Some are made commercially, but you can use a board propped on the stairs or on some bricks. Both legs can be stretched at the same time. Read a book for a while using this stretch.

STRETCHES FOR THE LOWER AREA OF THE HAMSTRINGS

This stretch is an excellent one for the hamstrings, using any object for support. Remember that your starting flexibility is unimportant; regular stretching will gradually increase your range. Start with a low support, like the seat of a chair. When you can touch your chin to your knee, use a higher object. Both knees should be kept straight.

This stretch is similar to the preceding one, but no support is required. This is an easy variation of one of the standard yoga asanas. In the asana, *the chin touches the knee, and the forearms are extended up the spine, palms pressed together.*

This is my favorite stretch for the lower hamstrings, because it also stretches the flanks, the spine, and the neck. This is the standard yoga triangle pose. Look up at your thumb. At first your lower arm will probably not reach your foot; slide it slowly down the leg. As you become more flexible you can touch the ground and then flatten your palm against the ground.

STRETCH FOR THE UPPER HAMSTRING AREA AND THE HIP

Note that the preceding stretches concentrate the tension low down at the back of the thigh. This stretch extends the muscles nearer the hip. Lie on your back, raise your leg as shown, and grasp it with both hands, pulling back gently. The idea is to move the leg as a unit, not to put leverage on the knee.

STRETCHING THE FRONT OF THE LEG

This stretch can be done lying down, as shown, or standing up with a wall or a car for support, if necessary. It is best to do it in bare or stockinged feet, since the Achilles pad of the shoe will often press against the tendon if you are wearing shoes. Grab your forefoot and bend the leg at the knee, concentrating on stretching the top of the foot and the front of the lower leg. Be cautious if you have a knee injury. Proceed to the next stretch.

After stretching the front of the lower leg, partially straighten your knee and move your arm farther back, so that you feel powerful stretching in the quadriceps muscles. Then repeat the whole sequence with the opposite leg.

STRETCHES FOR THE BACK

This is a simple but effective stretch for the back. Simply get on all fours and round the spine upward, concentrating on bending it into a smooth curve. Maintain the position and try to relax the muscles along the spine at the same time.

Bending your back downward reverses the previous stretch. Stretch well but gently in this position. If you have been having serious back pain or have a history of back trouble, don't do this stretch *or any other that bends the spine backward without consulting a doctor. Bending the spine backward can aggravate some back conditions.*

This stretch is a good one for the muscles of the torso and the spine. It also stretches the hamstrings. Lock your arm in front of the bent knee and straighten your arm to push yourself around. When this stretch becomes easy for you, bend the lower leg under you first and sit on it. Then put the other leg in the same position shown and do the stretch. Repeat in the opposite direction.

CHAPTER 10

Special Stretches and More Advanced Routines

T HIS CHAPTER includes a few additional stretches that may be useful for the runner who has particular problems or who wants to work on a few slightly more demanding stretches. If you want to undertake a more serious program, the yoga book mentioned earlier is suggested.

Note that many areas of the body will respond well to stretching if you find that you are becoming tight and cramped after a long run. Rolling the head around stretches the neck, rolling the trunk slowly at the waist will stretch your torso, and so on. Stretching the feet and ankles is always worthwhile, and it is easily done by sitting down, picking up one foot, and stretching it in various directions, following the usual principles. As we will see in Chapter Fourteen, this is very important for rehabilitation of a sprained ankle.

STRETCHING THE BACK

Rolling back and forth on the spine is an excellent way to relax and stretch the back. At first you should use a soft rug or a pad. The idea is to roll back very slowly, inch by inch, and then return the same way. You will find at first that you will roll very fast onto a flat spot in your spine. By concentrating on rounding it and rolling slowly, you will learn to stretch the stiff places in your spine.

This position, one of the many variations of the standard yoga plough pose, is an excellent way to stretch the back and hamstrings. Be careful at first, since the weight of the legs permits you to exert a lot of leverage. Relax, extend the position slowly, and learn to breathe easily in it. The spine can be curved more to flex the back or straightened out more to stretch the hamstrings.

A *more advanced method of bending the spine backward, the* cobra *pose. Look up, and stretch the spine starting with the head, which should reach for the sky. Relax the back muscles, and support yourself with the locked arms.* Do not attempt this pose without a physician's advice if you have chronic or severe back pain or a history of back trouble. *Bending the spine backward can aggravate some back problems.*

ADDITIONAL STRETCHES FOR THE FRONT OF THE LEGS

This stretch is superb for stretching the front muscles of the lower leg, the quadriceps, and the groin. Be cautious, and work into it slowly, however, because the use of body weight allows you to put a lot of leverage on the knee. When the bent leg is close in, as shown in the drawing, more stretch is exerted on the quadriceps. If you repeat the exercise with the leg farther out, you will stretch the groin more. You probably will not be able to let yourself all the way down at first; don't try to go too fast. Keep the knee of the bent leg on the ground.

A STRETCH FOR THE HAMSTRINGS AND THE GROIN MUSCLES

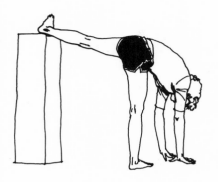

A two-step stretch for the hamstrings and the groin. Start as shown in the first illustration. Many people won't be able to touch the ground at first. If you can't, just grab your leg. Pause, relax, and stretch farther, as usual. Then bend your knee, as shown in the second illustration. This will shift the stretch to the groin of the raised leg. Repeat on the other side.

These stretches are excellent for stretching the back and all the muscles along the back of the legs. They are also good for muscle tone. The objective is the position shown in the third drawing, but don't try to achieve this at first. Start against the wall, as shown in the first illustration, gradually moving farther down the wall. Keep your legs straight and your kneecaps pulled up. Your feet should point straight ahead with your heels on the ground. Your back should be straight and relaxed. Work in front of a mirror at first, if possible. As you get better, use a low support, as in the center illustration. When you are ready to try the floor position, push up into it from a position on all fours.

Stretches to Relax the Arms and Shoulders

This stretch is good for limbering the muscles under the shoulder joint after or during a long run. The shoulders often tighten up toward the end of extended training runs. Stretching them out feels good and reduces cramping. Don't pull too hard in this stretch, since there is a lot of leverage on the joint.

Like the preceding stretch, this one is pleasant for relaxing the upper body muscles after or during distance training. Push the arms backward far enough for a comfortable stretch. This stretch also exerts a lot of leverage and should not be overdone.

CHAPTER 11

Special Exercises for Runners

MOST RUNNERS feel that they get plenty of exercise, and the attitude seems reasonable enough for an athlete putting in seventy-five miles on the roads and trails every week. Certainly running is one of the most efficient ways of exercising the cardiovascular system. But running develops mainly the muscles at the backs of the legs, leaving those at the front relatively weak—a condition that may result in overuse injuries or muscle pulls. Strengthening these muscles with special exercises is a good way to avoid injury at times when heavy demands are made on them, as in sprinting and hill climbing. Strengthening the quadriceps is also sometimes beneficial in dealing with knee problems, because the muscles are then better able to pull the kneecap into proper alignment.

Abdominal exercises are also important for runners, who usually have rather weak muscles there. This weakness can contribute to lower back pain. Reasonable abdominal strength is important to good physical conditioning, anyway, whether or not you are concerned about upper body strength in the arms and shoulders.

No specific upper body exercises are illustrated here. They are not relevant to injury prevention, and they also are the best known exercises. Push-ups, pull-ups, and dips between two chair backs make excellent conditioning exercises for the upper body, as do conventional weight exercises.

Unequal strength between the hamstrings of the two legs can result in muscle pulls, particularly among runners who are sprinting or doing speed work. If you are starting speed work, it is a good idea to visit a gym or someone with a good weight table that has a leg lever for the hamstrings. Test the relative strength of the hamstrings in the two legs. If one is significantly weaker, you should do weight work three times a week to bring it to the same strength as the stronger leg. This is an important part of rehabilitation after an injury. Recommencing hard training with a recently injured leg that's weak from disuse is a good way to pull the muscle again.

Exercises for the Feet and Ankles

Strengthening the feet and ankles is often very helpful in avoiding overuse injuries. Many of the syndromes that result from structural imperfections of the feet will not occur if the various muscles of the feet have been well developed. The abnormalities are still there; they just don't result in injuries as often. This is not difficult to understand, since the reason for an overuse injury is often simply that when the overworked muscles of the feet become tired, extra stress is placed elsewhere. Stronger muscles don't tire as quickly. Foot exercises won't always prevent injuries, but they often help.

There are dozens of possible foot exercises, and it's easy to devise more as a kind of game. The main difficulty is getting into the habit of doing them. A few are mentioned here as examples; make up your own. Rolling a round object like a Coke bottle back and forth while pressing down with the sole of the foot is good for the muscles there. Picking things up with your toes is excellent. If you work at it, you will find you can hold a pencil and write with the toes. They have a lot more dexterity than we normally develop. Laying out a towel on the floor, standing at one end, and gathering it all the way up with the toes is a good technique; when it gets easy, put a couple of bricks on the other end. Stand on the edge of a step barefoot with just your toes on the step, and raise yourself up several times.

BENT-LEG SIT-UPS

Regular sit-ups, in addition to being somewhat harder for most people than the bent-leg sit-up shown here, only exercise the abdominal muscles during part of the situp. Bent-leg sit-ups concentrate the work in the abdominal muscles. Bend your legs as shown, and roll your upper body up as far as shown in the illustration. Then slowly lower it again. If you do enough repetitions, you will find that bent-leg sit-ups are not as easy as they look. Do them often, rather than doing so many repetitions at a time that your stomach hurts.

Ankle exercises are just as easy to devise, often combining with foot exercises. Walking on the outside edges of your feet and then the inside edges is good. So is flexing your feet in every direction while resisting the motions with your hands.

EXERCISES TO STRENGTHEN THE QUADRICEPS

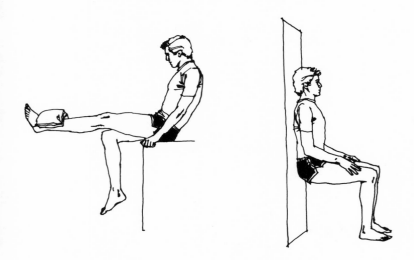

A good exercise to strengthen the quadriceps. Put a feed bag, a bag of bird seed, or a similar weight over the top of your foot while you sit on the edge of a table or ledge. Then raise your leg straight and repeat as many times as you comfortably can. Do the same number of repetitions with the other leg. Always start with the weaker leg.

Another good quadriceps exercise is to assume a sitting position with your back against the wall and no other support. At first you will probably either have to stay a little more upright or bend your knees a little under yourself. Work toward the position shown, with both joints at right angles. Hold as long as you comfortably can.

CHAPTER 12

Staying in Shape During a Layoff

T HE PSYCHOLOGICAL ASPECTS of any running injury are among the most difficult to deal with. Not all runners suffer physical withdrawal symptoms from lack of exercise, but most dedicated runners have made their daily runs an important part of their lives. When you are injured, you can't help but feel depressed over your inability to run, anxiously wondering whether you'll get over your ailment soon and whether the layoff is doing any good. Very often your incapacity to run has noticeable effects on your mood and your general physical state.

A lot of runners become irritable and nervous or have difficulty in sleeping when they have to stop running for a while. It is impossible to say how much of this is due to the physical need for the exercise and how much is caused by the deprivation of the psychological outlet that running provides. Some people are not affected this way at all and have little difficulty adjusting to spending an extra hour or two a day on other pursuits. Regardless of the need for running itself, however, most victims of injury are not happy about the prospect of losing their conditioning during the forced layoff following an injury.

Maintaining Cardiovascular Fitness

You will probably find that there is no satisfactory substitute for running. The special advantages and attractions that led you to it in the first place cannot be duplicated. Don't try to find a true substitute; it will only leave you dissatisfied. By comparing other activities to running, you'll make the time you spend at other pursuits less enjoyable, and you'll be less likely to continue them. The very fact that they have been injured makes many runners defensive about their running. They explain to friends and family why their substitute exercise is not nearly as good, becoming more depressed by the minute.

It makes a lot more sense to look positively at whatever alternative forms of recreation and exercise you choose. Your layoff can be an enjoyable experience or a somewhat traumatic one. You can get into shape for bicycle touring or bring your swimming ability up to a strong level. Instead of thinking how much you would rather be running, try to use the cardiovascular strength you have gained in running to allow you to progress rapidly in some interim activities that you don't normally have time to explore.

The most important type of conditioning for running, as well as for general good health, is that of the lungs, heart, and circulatory system. This is also the sort of fitness you can hope to maintain if you have to stop running for a time while an injury heals. Some of the conditioning that is specific to running, especially leg speed and tolerance to the mechanical stresses of high mileage is bound to be partially lost. When you are seriously injured, you have to resign yourself to this fact of life, but there is no reason why you can't maintain good cardiovascular fitness.

Those who want to retain a high level of conditioning may have to bring some real determination and imagination to the problem. One of the great advantages to running for exercise is its convenience. If you're lucky, another alternative might be just as handy at the time you need it, but there's a good chance that you won't be that fortunate. It is important to maintain perspective and common sense as well as determination in arranging alternatives. You may find, for example, that it is simply impossible to get in a good workout every day during your recuperation. This may be disheartening, but it is important to be flexible. A full workout every other day combined with some exercises in between will keep you in good condition. It is certainly better than becoming discouraged and dropping out altogether until you can run again.

Both practical considerations and the nature of your injury have to be taken into account in thinking about alternatives to running. Bicycling on a narrow-tired ten-speed bike will not be practical if the roads are rutted with ice and covered with snow and slush, or if you've pulled a quadriceps muscle. Often you will need to mix a number of activities to substitute for running because of various limiting factors. You might be able to swim for a short period each weekday during your lunch hour and take a long cross-country ski on one of the days of the weekend.

A number of possible activities provide a good cardiovascular workout. Bicycling, cross-country skiing, and swimming are the ones most comparable to running, but there are also good possibilities in rowing, paddling a canoe or kayak, walking, or working out with weights or calisthenics. Some of these alternatives are discussed in more detail below, but you can devise other ideas or combinations yourself. The essential ingredient is to elevate your heart rate enough so that you can retain your endurance. This can be done in many ways.

With some activities you may find at first that the stamina of the muscles used is not sufficient to allow you to exercise for a long period at a high energy output. For runners this is likely to be particularly true of sports that require a lot of power in the upper body. But persevere. You'll get stronger, just as you did in running. In the meantime a combination of activities will provide the duration of exertion you want. If your arms get tired from paddling, you can do a few calisthenics on shore while they rest, and then do another stint of paddling. Look on this recuperative period as a time to build some of the muscles that are neglected in running and to polish your technique in other sports.

Finally, don't get into the out-of-shape-American rut of justifying your lack of exercise and inactivity with excuses about needing equipment or with rationalizations concerning your schedule. If you *want* a workout, you'll get it. Do yoga. Do sit-ups and push-ups. Set up a friction device on a piece of nylon line, attach a couple of handles, and work your arms like a cross-country skier. Do calisthenics that don't require the use of your injured muscles or joints.

The great distance runner Emil Zatopek can stand as an example. He was unable to leave his house one night for his evening training run, so he ran in place in a bathtub filled with water and dirty clothes, doing the laundry at the same time. Zatopek also provides an example of the psychology of getting through a period without running. Just before the European championships in 1960, Zatopek had to spend two weeks in the hospital with a severe intestinal upset. His doctors and everyone else told him to forget the competition. He left for the games the day he got out of bed and won overwhelmingly in both the 5,000- and 10,000-meter races. I don't mean to advise you to try to race immediately after coming off an injury, but there is no need for excessive self-pity, either.

Bicycling

When it is feasible, bicycling is certainly one of the better substitutes for running. Like running, it relies mainly on the leg muscles, and you often can start from your doorstep rather than make a trip to a distant swimming pool or snow-covered slope.

The practical disadvantages of bicycling are likely to relate to the weather and time of year. In many areas winter cycling may simply be unreasonable, especially if there is a lot of traffic combined with narrow streets and snow. A distinction has to be made between commuting on a bike and riding hard enough to get a good workout. I find that it is practical to commute even in very nasty weather, but riding hard enough to provide really good exercise is difficult in winter. One has to be conservative when riding over icy patches and around cars that have limited visibility.

An old balloon-tire paper delivery bike is often better suited to exercise than a fine touring or racing bike. It's less vulnerable to the weather, it's stable in snow and ice, and you can get a workout even at slow speeds by cranking up to a high RPM and letting loose. If you can find one of these old classics in somebody's garage, you might start riding it to work and back. You may even decide to keep it up after your leg has healed.

Another difficulty with cycling during the fall and winter months is simply the availability of light. If you live in the northern part of the country, work during normal hours, and can't exercise at lunchtime, you won't be able to ride during the daylight hours. It's usually unsafe to ride at night; and even if you can find a safe location, it's pretty hard to work up much enthusiasm for a late-night bicycle ride. You may have to find another way to exercise, unless you can work out a way of riding to and from work. Even when part of your commuting is done in darkness, the necessity of the trip is often enough to make the plan psychologically practical—if you can find a reasonably safe route. Be sure to mount a reliable lighting system on your bike if you are planning to commute in poor light. Most of the commercial systems sold for bicycles are woefully inadequate. I use a motorcycle headlight and a strobe light at the rear with an amber lens, both wired to a rechargeable storage battery. Initial cost is high, but it works well and lasts indefinitely.

If your injury occurs during more reasonable weather, bicycling is a lot more attractive and easy to arrange. The attitude you take and the type of cycling you do can vary widely without affecting the value of the exercise. You can take out a good touring or racing bike and do some serious cycling, covering twenty-five to fifty miles in a workout lasting between one and two hours. But, you can also take out a three-speed utility bike or a single-speed clunker and manage to get an equally good workout for an hour or so. From the cyclist's point of view, the main disadvantages of less sophisticated bikes are that you can't travel nearly as far or as easily, and that if you ride for longer periods of time, you'll probably get sore from the upright position and the wide seat on the bike.

It's quite possible for just about anyone to get a good cardiovascular workout on a bike just by pedaling hard. An experienced cyclist usually has a somewhat lower output of energy than the runner unless the pace is very fast. This is true simply because the bicycle is a much more efficient way to travel, and the transitions in speed tend to be smoother. If you do a lot of cycling, you will probably have to work hard and do a lot of sprints to get as effective a two-hour workout as you would from running. The alternative is to take a longer ride.

Cycling is a smoother action than running, so overuse injuries in the legs are much less of a problem, and even the injured runner will often be able to cycle without difficulty. There are a few exceptions and qualifications, however. If you have a serious leg injury, you may have to do something that does not rely mainly on the legs, as cycling does. Pain can usually be used as a guide. If bicycling doesn't hurt, it is probably all right. Quadriceps pulls will probably preclude cycling because bicycling uses the quadriceps more than running does, especially if there are a lot of hills.

The effect of knee problems on cycling will vary, depending on where your trouble is. Talk to your physician, if you are under a doctor's care. In the long run bicycling can be beneficial in dealing with chondromalacia of the knee, because it strengthens the quadriceps, which then pull the kneecap into alignment a little more effectively. During the initial recovery phase from a knee injury, though, bicycling may be a poor idea. Overuse injuries of the tendons on the sides of the knees are due mainly to sideways stresses and may not be bothered by cycling. Whether or not your knees are hurt, you should learn to pedal rapidly on your bicycle rather than push very hard in a high gear, to avoid excessive stress on the knees.

Bicycling does not put nearly as much stress on the Achilles tendons as running does; but if you already have an Achilles injury, the normal pedaling position may strain them. If this is a problem, try pedaling with the flat of your foot, using no toe action, so that the Achilles are not used. If your bike is equipped with toe clips, they will have to be removed, or you will have to use the bottom of the pedals. The seat will also have to be lowered a little. Wearing hiking boots or other substantial shoes may help to take stress off the Achilles tendons. All this is bad bicycling technique, but you can still get good exercise. You just won't travel as far in the process.

For experienced cyclists who want the benefit of good cycling technique as well as exercise during a period of recovery from a running injury, there is one technique that may permit cycling with reduced stress on the Achilles and the rest of the legs. Try riding at a very high cadence (revolutions of the pedals per minute) while pushing a low gear. This reduces the stress on the legs, but increases the demand on the heart and lungs. It is also excellent training for cycling. A smooth, rapid cadence is the secret of both effective racing and long, effortless touring, and most cyclists will benefit from learning to speed up their legs.

Swimming

Swimming is another sport that can demand a very high energy output if it is done vigorously. It has the major advantage of putting little strain on many of the structures most frequently injured in running. If a standard kick disturbs an injury, you can swim using the upper body only and still work hard. Thus, no matter what the injury, swimming can always provide good exercise. Even leg damage that requires a cast does not have to put you out of commission if you request a Fiberglas cast, and the extra expense may be well worth bearing if you have to wear the cast for a long period.

For many people the major disadvantage of swimming is

the difficulty of getting access to a pool during hours when they are free. For some this problem may be insurmountable. For others it requires just a little perseverance and thought. YMCAs, YWCAs, municipal pools, schools, and private clubs may all provide possibilities. Pools that are part of apartment or townhouse complexes may also be available. Such pools often have the advantage of being open during odd hours, when they're likely to receive little use. The main problem with them is that they're often rather small, which is a nuisance when you're trying to swim hard. When making turns in a small pool, don't kick off. This will increase the number of strokes you have to use to swim the length of the pool. In public pools the ideal time is usually one reserved for adults to swim laps, rather than a general family period, when the pool is often crowded with people going in every direction. These are minor annoyances, though, and with a little patience you can get a workout any time you have access to a pool.

Another disadvantage of swimming is that you may have difficulty getting a full workout if your technique is bad or has deteriorated. Most of us who don't swim regularly suffer from muscle fatigue and poor coordination long before we have worked hard for an hour. If you can swim, though, just keep trying. You'll find that if you swim every day for a couple of weeks, you will improve by leaps and bounds. You will also gain a worthwhile skill and a lot of upper-body strength in the process.

Cross-Country Skiing

Cross-country skiing is a superb exerciser for those recuperating from moderate overuse injuries. The motions involved are smooth enough not to aggravate many running injuries. The energy output required by hard cross-country skiing is very high. As in swimming, the upper body and legs are both used, so the energy demands can actually be greater than in running. The disadvantages are also fairly obvious. Snow and equipment have to be accessible, and you need good technique to be able to work hard for any period of time. Equipment can now be rented fairly easily in most parts of the country where there is enough snow, but technique takes some time for the complete beginner to acquire. If there is enough snow, mountains or extensive trails are not required. You can set a track in a local park and ski around it hard.

The utility of cross-country skiing for training during a layoff is limited mainly to those with moderate overuse injuries who are already familiar with the sport, but it can be a boon for them. If you are a good cross-country skier, you can even do poling training with roller skis during the off-season, but this is an option that will be practical for only a few runners.

Rowing and Paddling

Like cross-country skiing, rowing any craft or paddling a canoe or a kayak can be an excellent endurance exercise, but is limited to those with access to the necessary equipment. You may also need a certain amount of skill to begin with. The basic coordination necessary to use a rowboat could be picked up in a short enough time by anyone, but this is not true of rowing shells, kayaks, and canoes. With these crafts some basic competence is required to enable you to work hard without embarking on a course of self-destruction. On the other hand, these sports rely heavily on upper-body strength, so they are not likely to be limited by any running injury. They are mentioned here partly to suggest the wide variety of possible substitutes for running in maintaining cardiovascular fitness.

Walking

The humble art of walking deserves a lot more attention and respect from runners, both as a part of their normal training and as a part of the recuperative process. The degree of vigor that can be put into walking is not recognized by most people these days, even runners. Few individuals in the United States do much walking at all, because the country is centered around the automobile. When we do take to our feet, we stroll rather than walk at a brisk pace. Those of us who have taken up running are in a hurry, like everyone else, and we want our exercise in concentrated doses.

There are many ways to walk, but to establish the value of walking for conditioning, let's start off by mentioning race walking. Good race walkers can maintain a pace of around eight minutes per mile for long periods. This is the pace for a 3½-hour marathon, a good deal faster than a lot of runners achieve, so it is well to think twice before you dismiss walking as an exercise.

Race walking itself is a refined art, and the rules require a specialized technique that will not be covered here. If you concentrate on walking vigorously, however, you will find that you can get a surprisingly good workout. Even those with fairly disabling running injuries can often walk hard after a good warm-up without aggravating their problems. You may learn a lot in the process, too, because when you are covering very long training distances in running, the most effective technique is often to drop to an occasional walk.

For non-race walkers, getting a good workout will generally take a little longer than it does when you're running, but there are some advantages that may offset this inconvenience. The lower work level may make it more practical to combine your exercise with getting to or from work or with necessary errands. Fewer changes of clothes may be required, and you may not have to worry about the logistics of showering and changing, as you do after running. These factors may even make the total time required for a hard walk less than that required for a run.

As an additional benefit you may find later on that walking makes an excellent regimen for days following a hard running workout, when your legs are still tired from the day before. Walking has many of the benefits of running without imposing nearly as much stress on the joints and tendons. Like running, it is a lost art that needs to be revived.

Weight Training and Calisthenics

No detailed recommendations for weight training will be included here. Much will depend on the facilities you have available and on your own circumstances and desires. It is important to point out, however, that not all weight training or calisthenics have to be directed toward increasing absolute muscle strength. The best way to increase the size of your muscles and your maximum strength is to lift large weights a few times or to work against heavy resistance.

For endurance and cardiovascular development the ideal is the opposite. You want to work against a small resistance rapidly and for many repetitions. Thus if you want to get good endurance exercise, it would be better to do thirty repetitions with fifty pounds, then twenty-five bent-leg sit-ups, then another thirty weight repetitions, and so on, instead of pressing 150 pounds five or six times and then stopping for five minutes to catch your breath. The precise routines and the type of exercise can be varied and may not include weights at all. It is the principle of many repetitions at a moderate load that is important.

For example, most runners would find it difficult to do

many conventional push-ups or sit-ups, because their upper body strength is not highly developed. It would be far preferable to do several sets of push-ups pivoting from your knees rather than your toes, alternating with other types of exercise, so that the demand on your heart and lungs is kept high. With a little thought you can easily work out a combination that will enable you to keep in condition anywhere.

Working Back into Running Without Getting Hurt

If you do maintain a really high level of fitness during a period of injury, it's particularly important to work back into running *gradually*. You may be able to prevent any loss of overall conditioning through swimming or cycling, but the tendons and joints of your legs will not be able to tolerate a maximum running load for some time. This would be true even if you had not been injured. There is a tremendous psychological need to work very hard and get back up to form after an injury. It is vital to resist this temptation and to realize that it will take some time to return to your previous capacity. Rushing things will simply make another injury likely.

Pay particular attention to stretching, warm-ups, base running, and taking easy days. Leg speed usually takes some time to return; and even if you can manage to run fast right away, your legs will often not be able to withstand the stress. Plan on twice the length of the layoff to return to your former level of running after a mild injury, and four times its length after a severe one.

Part III

ACCIDENTS, HEAT, AND COLD

CHAPTER 13

Avoiding Accidental Injuries

ACCIDENTAL INJURIES pose a far less insidious threat to the runner than the products of overstress. They are much less common, and the dangers are usually obvious, so that they seem easier to deal with. In the case of traffic hazards, however, the danger is infinitely more serious. Frustrating as stress fractures and tendonitis may be, the consequences are not in the same category as being run down by a pickup truck doing seventy miles an hour. Most road runners become far too blasé about the dangers of traffic. Familiarity breeds contempt, but it behooves us to remind ourselves occasionally how easy it is to be badly hurt by a careening automobile.

Other accidental injuries that can occur to runners are less common and less serious than those posed by motorists. But they are just as painful as overuse injuries, interfere just as much with training, and so deserve some attention. A bad sprain sustained on a trial run can make running impossible for quite a long time. Accidental injuries lack the nagging frustration of many overuse injuries at their onset, but they are just as debilitating once they have been sustained.

Dealing with Traffic

By far the best recipe for handling traffic is to avoid it altogether. If there is a suitable network of good trails near your home, it will provide a more pleasant running environment than the roads and city streets. There are a number of other side benefits as well. Trail running is far less likely to produce many of the overuse injuries that result from running constantly on hard pavement. Trails with poor surfaces may increase the likelihood of a sprain or a twisted knee, but even these are no worse hazards than potholes or oncoming cars.

Parks and tracks with relatively soft surfaces also provide possibilities if they fit in with your running style and training distances. Golf courses may also be good running courses, if you can avoid official conflicts and run at a time when the golfers aren't about.

For most of us, however, there are serious problems with all these alternatives, at least during some parts of the year, and we are forced out onto the roads. Some people don't really mind running on a track or around a small park, school grounds, or some similar spot. There is no doubt that you always *can* run in such places, and serious runners should find a safe place to use at least on those occasions when the roads are exceptionally dangerous. But for most of us who run long distances every day, repeated track sessions are a colossal bore. The point is not that we can't make ourselves run on the track every day, but that we don't want to. Running through different and varied surroundings is a lot more fun. Trails are always interesting; but even where they are available, they often become impossible to use during much of the year.

Near my own home, for example, there is a fine network of trails that are my favorite running routes. They are quite rough, however, strewn with rocks and full of holes, with lots of steep stretches. Even when they are not dangerously icy or sufficiently snow-covered to conceal bad footing, they are far too hazardous for running in the dark. During much of the year it is simply impossible to make my entire run during daylight hours. Either I start in the dark or I finish that way, so I end up on the roads at the most dangerous times of the year. Most runners are not fortunate enough to have trails to use even during the summer months. Road running thus becomes a virtual necessity.

The cardinal safety rule for running the roads is to pay constant attention whenever there is traffic and to assume

The dangers of traffic present the most severe hazard for runners who train on the roads.

that the driver of every car is some sort of lunatic. You'll be surprised to find how often this assumption is correct. Never depend on a driver stopping at a light or a stop sign, looking in your direction before bombing out of an intersection or driveway, or giving you your legal right-of-way.

The first fact of life that the road runner has to deal with is that motorists are often unaware of pedestrians. A driver will simply not see you; his eyes may register your presence in patterns of light, but they aren't picked out from the surroundings by his mind. Much of the skill of driving is in the ability to filter out those features of the motorist's surroundings that are irrelevant to the operation of the car. If the driver is looking at the birds flying by or the mountains in the background, he won't notice the subtle signs that tell him an approaching car is about to pull in front of him.

Unfortunately for the runner, drivers have almost universally trained themselves to view the pedestrian as completely irrelevant to the operation of a vehicle. You might as well be a hedge or a roadside rock for the amount of attention you will receive from the average driver. It is important that we all work to change this situation, but in the meantime you'd better concentrate on surviving it.

Even if a driver notices your presence, you should realize that he will consider you to be an essentially stationary object. A driver about to make a left turn across your path may see you a half a block before, but he will not register the fact that you are traveling fast enough to be in front of his car by the time he makes the turn. Drivers are trained to allow for the motion of other cars in guiding their own, but they do not consider the possibility of rapid motion by people on foot.

For these reasons it is essential to be very careful in crossing at intersections, exits from shopping centers and businesses, and similar spots. In any case where a car may be crossing your path, don't expose yourself until you are *positive* the driver sees you and is going to stop. Cars coming from side roads and turning right onto a main street are particularly dangerous. The driver will typically slow or stop while looking to his left at the oncoming traffic, and then pull out without ever looking to the right. If you continue running along a sidewalk or the edge of the street assuming the driver will stop, you are likely to be run down. Knocking on the hood to get the driver's attention before you cross is often an effective expedient.

A less common danger—but one that is harder to anticipate—comes from cars making left turns. If you are running against traffic and crossing a side street or a business entrance, a driver coming from behind you on the other side of the street will often keep his eye on the approaching traffic and run right into you. It is important to be alert to this possibility, because you have to look over your shoulder to see cars in these circumstances.

These two examples should be sufficient to make the main point: You have to rely on your own attentiveness in traffic to keep from being seriously injured by a car. The same precept applies to country roads and highway shoulders, particularly in conditions of poor visibility.

Making Yourself Visible

Given the fact that drivers are rarely on the lookout for runners and habitually pay little attention to them, making yourself as visible as possible when you are running the roads is a simple principle of self-preservation. My instinctive taste in running clothes gravitates naturally toward the unobtrusive—modest blues, greens, and grays. But it makes a lot more sense to be flamboyant in your choice of running gear for the roads. Pick the loudest clothing you can stand, particularly when poor light or bad weather makes you hard to see. A runner wearing dark clothes on a rainy night is pretty difficult for even a well-meaning driver to pick out, so it really pays to be sensible in this area. Light clothing stands out a lot better in most situations. White is good except on snow.

At dusk and dawn bright clothes are particularly helpful, combined with a healthy respect for the things that a *driver* can see. The reflective devices discussed below are worthless until cars turn their lights on, and they are less effective when the sky is light, even if a driver does have his headlights on. A dawn and dusk the sky is quite bright, but objects on the ground are not well lighted. The driver's pupils adjust to the light intensity coming from above and often cannot pick out objects on the road. Even a good reflector does not show up well in the glare of headlights. Bright colors like yellow, orange, and chartreuse are a help in attracting the driver's attention.

It is also important to remember that the glare from the sun may blind the oncoming driver. When the sun is at your back, it is right in the driver's eyes, and there is a very good chance that you will not be seen. Be prepared to dodge.

At night white clothing is a help, but the most effective protection comes from a combination of alertness and reflective devices. Modern reflectors show up very brightly in the headlights of an automobile. The next time you are out driving on a dark road at night, note how much sooner you see reflective signs than anything near them, including white signposts. Unlike lights, reflectors need no attention or maintenance once you have attached them to the clothing you wear for running after dark. Reflective bands on the arms and legs are particularly effective, because the eccentric motion of the lights seen by the motorist attracts his attention. There are commercially produced vests, arm and leg bands, and warm-up suits with reflective trim that is unobtrusive during the day. If you can find the fabric, it's quite easy to make your own.

Defensive Running

We have already touched somewhat on the importance of defensive running for safety around cars, but it is important on roads with few cars as well as in the traffic of cities and towns. Drivers on back roads are often less attentive than those in town. They are likely to drive at high speed whether or not they can see the roadway ahead. Runners are also more likely to relax their guard when running back roads. After you've hit your stride, it's easy to drop into a trancelike state or to become so involved with the scenery or the feeling of running that you become oblivious to the pickup coming over the rise. To maintain a reasonable margin of safety, it is important to remain aware of what is going on around you.

It is usually better to run against traffic, unless there is a sidewalk or a rather large path separated from the main roadway. You are bound to encounter people who will nearly run you down, and if you are facing them, you'll notice them in time to dive for the dirt when necessary.

If the roads where you run have a pronounced crown, so that the edge of the road tilts, the constant effect of the slanted surface on your feet and legs may cause injuries. If the traffic is light enough and your visibility is very good, you can sometimes switch back and forth to stay on the opposite side of the road from passing cars. Switching has the advantages of keeping you well out of the way of cars and of changing the stress on your legs. You may even be able to run the center of the road and move to the appropriate side as a car approaches, but this is far too dangerous except in ideal circumstances.

Defensive running is most important at night and during poor weather. Most of us who run year-round have no choice but to run in the dark during the winter months. It is important to recognize how dangerous this can be, however, and to choose running routes that are reasonably safe. It is vital that you realize that some drivers just won't see you at night, though reflective clothing will improve your odds enormously. Try to find routes away from the roads, streets with very little traffic, or at least roads with good shoulders. The time to run narrow roads with poor footing at the edges is not at night or during a snowstorm. If you should have to dodge a car, you want to be able to run off the road without spraining an ankle.

Footing and Shoe Stability

Except for traffic, hazards to runners are not nearly as serious as those in many other sports. The worst accidental injury you are likely to sustain is a sprained ankle. It is an obvious corollary to Murphy's Law, however, that if you do hurt your ankle, it will happen just as you are peaking for a big marathon. (Murphy's Law states that anything that can go wrong will, always at the worst possible time.)

The most obvious danger of spraining an ankle, twisting a knee, or sustaining a similar mishap comes from poor footing. A pothole in the street that you don't notice, a rock in the trail, or any similar obstacle can cause a sprain or fracture. The only direct method of prevention is to watch where you are going. There are important secondary causes, however.

Runners don't usually get sprains and broken bones when they are fresh. You are far more likely to be alert when you're not tired. Your muscles also have the reserve strength to recover from most missteps. When you're not tired, a certain slip may result in nothing more than broken rhythm, but the same slip may cause a broken ankle when you begin to flag. You are also far more likely to trip and fall when you're tired, especially on rough trails. Your antigravity muscles—the ones you use to lift your legs—usually succumb to fatigue first, and you are likely to catch a foot on an obstacle that projects slightly from the trail. Be extra careful of your footing when you're tired, and avoid rough trails if possible at the end of a long run, especially if the light is failing.

Less obvious contributors to accidental turns, sprains, and fractures may be your shoes. If you do much running in places with poor footing, it is as important to consider the stability of your shoes as it is to consider cushioning. Stability on trails riddled with rocks and irregularities is not the same as stability on a track or on pavement. A good trail shoe has to hold your foot when you run on sidehills and other non-level spots. Many shoes that give excellent foot support for road runners are dreadful trail shoes. Wide soles should not always be ruled out, but they are definitely not helpful in foot placement on rough terrain. They may tend to twist your foot to one side or to catch on rocks that a narrower sole would pass without difficulty. If you do much running on irregular ground, try putting a lot of twisting force on the shoes when you try them on in the store, to get a feeling for the way they will act on trails. Avoid shoes that tend to throw your ankle over when the sole strikes the ground at an angle.

Dogs and Their Owners

Dogs are often a plague to runners, though not usually one that threatens serious injury. A dog nipping at your heels is a major annoyance and certainly one you shouldn't have to put up with, but it is usually possible to avoid a bite. Even if you get one—providing you don't have to have rabies shots as a result (see below)—it is rarely bad enough to require even a day's layoff.

Ideally, though, it's better to keep from being bitten in the first place. And anything you can do to discourage future attacks is nice, too. Try a friendly verbal greeting to the dog first, but be prepared to make a more substantial defense if necessary. The usual remedy is a well-placed fusillade of rocks. Most dogs that go after runners are quite familiar with having rocks tossed at them, and they will often retreat at the first motion of your arm. If you see a loose dog ahead, it's always a good idea to collect a few rocks just in case. Even if you're caught off guard, the mere pretense of throwing stones will often make the dog flee. Never turn your back on a mean dog. Most dogs are cowards when they aren't protecting their owners or doorsteps, and they'll only bite a runner from behind.

In case of real problem dogs on a regular running route, complaints to the authorities are the appropriate remedy. Unfortunately, this often turns out to consume vast amounts of time and energy with no effect at all. Often it is more effective to carry a can of Mace or Halt (the repellent that cyclists and mail carriers use) or a spray bottle of ammonia on a few runs. If you make a point of hitting every vicious dog on your route with one of these, you'll usually find that they won't bother you again. The idea of a Mace run is to chase the dogs that usually go after you and make sure to spray them. The real culprits are the owners, of course, but the law frowns on walking up to a door and squirting Mace at an owner when you are attacked by his dog.

All the preceding comments apply only to dogs that are instinctively trying to nip you because they don't like runners or are protecting what they feel is their territory. If you should happen to encounter a trained attack dog on your route and survive the experience, don't go back until the dog has been taken care of in some way. There are a few psychopaths around who keep such animals in places where they can get out. If you are actually attacked by one, it will leap for your throat. The standard technique is to feed him your forearm to protect your neck, place your other arm behind the dog's neck, and then bend his head backwards with a quick snap. Fortunately, you are not likely to encounter one of these dogs.

Some dog owners, if they are nearby, will become violently angry if you throw a rock at their dear Fang, feeling that his trying to chew through your Achilles tendon is not sufficient excuse to justify violence on your part. Don't try to argue with this type of nut; just leave as quickly as you can.

Rabies and Infection

The biggest danger from animal bites is rabies, a disease that attacks the central nervous system. It is quite deadly, and there is no safe vaccine for humans. If you receive a bite from a potentially rabid animal, the standard procedure is for the health authorities to confine the animal to see whether it has contracted rabies. If the animal cannot be found, you have to undergo a series of painful and dangerous injections, because successful treatment is usually not possible once the disease becomes manifest. This is why it is very important that the animal be identified and captured if you receive any bite that breaks the skin.

Rabies is fairly common in a number of species of wild animals and can easily be transmitted to pets that have not been recently vaccinated. Since rabies often (but not always) causes abnormal behavior in its later stages, a biting animal may well be rabid—the disease causes the unusual behavior of attacking a person. If at all possible, the animal should be captured alive; but if it is killed, the head must be preserved for examination by public health specialists. Don't take an owner's word that an animal has been vaccinated; call the police if you are bitten. Rabies can be transmitted by animals other than dogs, but dogs present the primary danger for runners.

Any animal bite carries a strong danger of infection, quite aside from the danger of rabies, because of the large number of bacteria present in the saliva. If you are treating a bite yourself, it must be thoroughly cleansed, preferably scrubbed with a brush. Any deep punctures or signs of infection should prompt you to seek medical attention.

Protecting Your Eyes

One hazard that most runners ignore but is potentially quite serious is the danger of eye injury from low-hanging branches. Even in good light, it is quite possible to miss a small twig when you are coming around a corner or dodging a larger branch. It is very easy to do in dark or twilight conditions, when small branches are very hard to see. Woodland trails are naturally most dangerous, but quite a few city sidewalks have low-hanging branches, too. You may not notice any of these when running normally in good light; but if your attention is distracted or you are running at dusk, you can seriously hurt an eye.

The best way to avoid this sort of problem is to take mental note of the trees and bushes that might pose a danger on a day when visibility is good. Then when you run in poor light conditions, you will know where to be careful.

Ice

Cold weather itself doesn't create any danger for the runner, as long as enough clothing is worn and some care taken.

(Normal precautions for cold weather are discussed in Chapter Fourteen.) Icy roads and walks can present real problems, however, and should be approached with caution. Ice can be a direct hazard, because it's easy to slip when running, and an indirect hazard if there is traffic to contend with. Car drivers have poor control and are usually driving with reduced visibility at the same time.

Avoid icy roads unless they are completely free of traffic. Running anywhere near cars in slippery conditions is just too dangerous. The drivers probably won't see you, and even if they do, they may not be able to avoid you. You're better off making fifty rounds of a small park.

Icy patches can also cause slips and possible broken bones, especially if there is little snow to break your fall. Older runners in particular may want to avoid the risk of a bruising fall on those occasions when the streets and sidewalks are very slick. A track or a grassy area is more likely to have reasonable footing in icy conditions. Running through snow will give you a good workout, and your feet usually won't get cold when you're running unless there is a lot of cold water underneath. If no safe route is available, you may be better off skipping a workout than running on slippery streets.

The trick of running on ice and packed snow is to achieve the speed you want by increasing your tempo rather than your kick. Run lightly with your center of gravity solidly over your feet. You won't be able to get a really strong push-off from the toe, but you can easily get a lot of work on leg speed. By avoiding fast starts, stops, and corners, you can often run on icy surfaces fairly well.

CHAPTER 14

Sprains, Breaks, and Wounds

C OMPARED to many other sports participants, runners do not take very large risks of accidental injury. Running involves no body contact and little activity that puts sideways stress on the joints, so the risk of injuries of the kind typical in football, basketball, and similar sports is almost nil. Still, many runners are out on the roads, trails, and tracks for an hour or two every day, covering five to fifteen miles. With so much running you're bound to occasionally twist an ankle or a knee. Such accidental traumatic injuries are the subject of this chapter.

Wounds

Unless you are hit by a car, you are unlikely to sustain any serious wounds while running. A slip or collision with a branch may result in an abrasion or a cut, but these are no different from those mishaps encountered in any other activity of life. The important rule in dealing with minor wounds is to wash them thoroughly and keep them clean. Cuts and abrasions left open to the air form dry scabs quickly and heal well, so this is usually the best treatment for wounds that don't require dressings to insure cleanliness or protection from abrasion.

Puncture wounds are always somewhat dangerous, because of the added danger of infection. It is difficult for the body to clean a puncture and hard to wash it effectively. And punctures are most likely to occur in the feet, which are especially hard to keep clean. Debris from construction or from old buildings often contains protruding nails that can be covered with leaves or other loose material, so that it is easy to step on them. The soles of running shoes don't present much resistance to punctures.

It is usually advisable to go to a doctor if you receive a puncture wound, particularly if it doesn't bleed profusely. It isn't a bad idea to finish your run first, simply to stimulate bleeding before the wound stiffens and becomes too painful to permit a lot of motion. A reasonable amount of bleeding is the best guarantee that bacteria and dirt will be washed out of a puncture wound. Make sure your tetanus boosters are up to date if you receive a puncture wound.

Sprains

Sprains are the most likely accidental injuries to runners. You are bound to step occasionally in a pothole or on the edge of a hidden rock and turn your ankle a bit. Most such injuries are so minor that they don't even stop you from running, but some can be quite serious. It's not always easy to tell one from the other, and even a physician may require a number of X rays before making a positive diagnosis of the extent of the damage. Since you have to decide what to do for yourself, however, there are several rules of thumb worth remembering.

One characteristic of many injuries, especially those to the joints, is that after the initial stab of pain when the twist occurs, there is an automatic anesthetic effect produced by the body, which dulls the pain considerably even in the case of many serious sprains and ligament injuries. Presumably, this masking of pain is the body's way of letting you get out of whatever fix you are in, and it must have been helpful in enabling our ancestors to survive. This lowered level of pain can be useful in allowing you to get home after sustaining a serious injury.

Of course, a lot of missteps don't cause any significant injury at all, and the pain disappears rapidly because nothing was really damaged. One danger of the anesthetic effect, however, is that it can lull you into believing that you are not seriously hurt even when you really are. It is important to test your leg very gingerly, since an injured joint will be seriously weakened, and you can very easily hurt it more by stressing it. The ankle or knee is likely to collapse at the slightest side pressure, resulting in a bad break or a rupture of tissue that was only slightly damaged before.

After turning an ankle even mildly, in fact, you should be very careful not to put much pressure on it in the bad direction, since it is likely to be at least temporarily weakened by the earlier strain. Unless you're sure that you haven't sustained any injury, you should head home after turning an ankle or knee and treat for a sprain. A few hours later you will have a much more realistic idea of how badly you are hurt.

Standard treatment for strains, sprains, and most other injuries is icing applied as soon after the injury as possible and continued intermittently for several hours. The reason is simple. In any injury in which there is tissue damage, blood vessels will be torn and injured. The injured blood vessels bleed into the surrounding tissue, causing the familiar swelling, the bruised color, and some of the pain and stiffness associated with the injury. Healing is retarded by the collected blood, which takes some time to dissipate. Cold treatment of the injured area has an anesthetic effect and also reduces bleeding and the resultant swelling. It is almost universally helpful in treating running injuries.

Real sprains should not be taken lightly. Any ankle injury or turned knee that still is giving you pain or is swollen or weak in any direction after icing for twenty minutes when you get home should be examined by a doctor. If it does not seem serious, you may choose to wait twenty-four hours before seeing a physician, but you should see one. Ligament or bone damage is often present in sprains that do not seem too severe, and improper treatment can result in unnecessary long-term problems.

In the case of bad breaks or dislocations the damage and the need to seek medical help will be obvious. In these unusual cases the only problem that may arise is getting to a doctor or a hospital. If you run on little-used trails, you should consider this possibility, particularly in cold weather. Don't walk on a seriously injured leg unless it is a matter of survival.

It is more difficult to decide when a turned ankle requires medical attention and when it is not really of any consequence. I would advise sitting down for a few minutes to collect your wits whenever you turn an ankle or a knee, even in the most minor way. It is easy to turn an ankle mildly, try to keep running, and then twist it again—more severely—because of the short-term weakness caused by the first misstep. Stopping for a few minutes prevents this sort of accident and gives you time to find out whether the injury will get better or worse.

After sitting for a couple of minutes, test the injured leg gingerly to find out how it feels, whether there is any lingering weakness, and whether there is pain simply from bearing weight. If there seems to be no serious weakness and not much pain, start walking. You should not have to limp badly; if you do, you have sustained more than a trivial injury. If the turn was only mild, you should be able to walk the pain off completely in five minutes or so. A lot of pain or pronounced limping indicates more critical damage, and you should get home to ice the area. Even if the pain disappears, don't continue to run on rough ground unless you are *sure* there is no lingering weakness. Even the slightest remaining aftereffect from the misstep can be enough to cause serious injury later in the run. It is better to get onto flat ground and to do your running on level surfaces for a few days.

Remember that in the case of serious pain that doesn't go away, it is best not to walk or run on your injured leg if you can avoid it. If you can hitch a ride home, do so. If you have a friend along on a run, have him get a car or help you to the nearest road.

Getting Over a Sprain

The advisability of seeing a doctor about any sprain that is still causing pain, forcing a limp, or showing any serious swelling or instability after you get home and ice the injury has already been mentioned. You should consult with the doctor about rehabilitating the injured area as well. After any serious sprain a lot of stretching and exercising will be necessary to regain good strength and flexibility. This may require quite a bit of work and time if the sprain was serious enough to require casting. You should get medical advice on the techniques needed after serious sprains in either the knee or the ankle.

Often, though, the doctor will x-ray a sprained ankle, determine that the damage has been relatively minor, and send you home. Once the swelling has gone down, you should begin flexing the ankle and doing exercises. The more you can strengthen the ankle, the better off you will be, because an ankle is always weaker after a sprain, making later injuries much more likely. When you are stretching and exercising your ankle, be extremely careful about flexing it in the direction in which the sprain took place, since ligaments heal slowly. But don't neglect gentle flexing exercises. They are essential if you want to regain full motion in the ankle.

To exercise and stretch the ankle, I prefer to sit on a chair and cross the injured leg over the good one. The foot can then be grasped with the hands and gently moved in every direction to improve flexibility. The muscles in the ankle, foot, and leg should be used to push the foot slowly against the hands in each possible direction. Repeat all the actions several times during each session. All the foot exercises mentioned in Chapter Eleven can also be used beneficially.

Taping

Once your ankle is in reasonably good shape and you are ready to start running on it again, you may want to tape it before running until you are sure that it will withstand any accidental sideways force. Don't use tape to allow you to run on an ankle that is still injured, especially if you have been advised by a doctor not to run yet. Taping is very useful, however, after the ankle is essentially healed, to reinforce ligaments that may still be too weak to withstand accidental sideways deformation. (See high Dye strapping p. 234.)

Though there are a number of subtle types of damage that can occur in the ankle, basic classification is fairly simple. The ankle joint itself permits movement only in one plane. The ends of the two bones of the lower leg, the tibia and the fibula, form the large protrusions you can feel on either side of your ankle. These sit on the sides of the anklebone like a rider with two legs on either side of a saddle. The foot can move up and down on this joint, but has very limited sideways motion. Ligaments bind the joint on either side to guard against displacement in case of a strong sideways force, though the weight of the body normally holds the leg bones firmly astride the ankle joint. In the case of a sprain, the foot is bent strongly to one side, and the ligaments on the outside of the bend are torn.

The great majority of sprains are so-called *inversion sprains*, damaging the outer ligaments of the ankle as the foot is bent inward, so that the sole of the foot faces the other leg. About a quarter of all ankle sprains are on the inside, caused when the foot bends outward, with the sole facing away from the other leg. The technical name is an *eversion sprain*.

The idea of taping is to use the tensile strength of the tape to replace or supplement the weakened structures of the body. To reinforce a sprained ankle, the tape should hold the injured side of the ankle to prevent it from exceeding its normal range of motion. In the majority of cases most of the tape should be on the outside of the ankle to supplement the ligaments there. If the sprain was the less common one on the inside of the ankle, most of the taping should be there.

There are several techniques for taping ankles. Many of those used with participants in contact sports like football nearly immobilize the ankle. These methods may be appropriate for a runner during the recovery stage after an ankle injury, but you should not return to running if your ankle needs this much support. A lot of stress will be put on the skin if you try, and the taping job will lose much of its strength after a couple of miles on the road, anyway. Don't go back to running until you can do so with a fairly natural gait. Besides hurting the ankle itself, a radically altered stride will probably cause you to sustain overuse injuries some-where else in your legs.

The taping methods appropriate for distance runners are designed to allow the foot to move fairly naturally but prevent sideways motion beyond what the ligaments should normally allow. The tape may also support the foot somewhat if it tends to roll over excessively, a weakness that may have helped cause the sprain to begin with. I think the simplest and most useful aid for the runner is the high Dye strap, devised by the doctor of the same name. Because the method is derived from a taping technique also used for foot support, it is shown in the taping drawings in Chapter Eighteen.

CHAPTER 15

Cold-Weather Injuries

As LONG AS a few reasonable precautions are taken, cold weather is not really hazardous to runners. The greatest danger is really from traffic, since drivers have less control of their cars in conjunction with reduced visibility. A motorist peering through a small clear patch in the windshield is not likely to see a runner at the periphery of his vision. These problems were discussed in detail in Chapter Twelve. With a little prudence in choosing routes, waiting for cars to pass at intersections, and the like, you can run safely through the nastiest winter.

Flu and Colds

One caveat I think you should follow is to avoid running in cold weather if you have a respiratory infection or are fighting one off. Cold air is often very dry. The air's humidity is further reduced as it is warmed in your respiratory passages. (Warm air can hold more water vapor than cold. This is why dew and frost condense when air is cooled. When the air is rewarmed, its relative humidity is quite low.) Thus the newly warmed air dries out the respiratory passages, which is not at all desirable when you have a cold or the flu.

For these reasons you are likely to come through the cold weather stronger and better trained if you don't try to run through colds or flu. You will usually recover faster and be able to return to training sooner if you don't try to run. If you get a bad runny nose and sore throat, it's usually best to wait a couple of days to see whether the infection will spread to the lungs before running in the cold.

Hypothermia

Hypothermia means chilling of the body core. It is a killer and can be a real hazard to runners who are careless in preparing for long cold-weather runs. The human body will function properly only if the vital organs are kept within a very narrow temperature range. A variation of a few degrees in the temperature of the central core of the body will first cause a rapid decline in efficiency, then total incapacity, and finally death.

The body has a highly efficient system of controls to maintain an even temperature in the essential organs of the trunk and head. When you begin to overheat—far more of a problem for runners than chilling—circulation is increased and the blood vessels near the surface of the body open wide, so that the blood can carry heat to the skin, where it can be dissipated. Sweating is used to obtain cooling by evaporation, so that the body can be kept cooler than the air around it even when you are working hard.

The runner produces so much waste heat during heavy exercise that this cooling system often goes into operation even when you are running in rather cold conditions. One effect can be that your clothes become soaked with sweat, and evaporative cooling may continue for some time, long after it has ceased to be desirable. (It requires a great deal of energy to change water from a liquid to a vapor, energy that is absorbed in the form of heat. As sweat evaporates from the skin, it absorbs heat and cools the skin.)

When the temperature of the body starts to drop, the regulatory system reacts in just the opposite way. Circulation to most of the skin is reduced, and the temperature of the surface of the body is allowed to drop, so that less heat will be lost to the environment. This is why your skin is often so cold when you come in from outdoors, even if you are not at all uncomfortable. If the body is still losing too much heat, circulation to the extremities is also reduced and your hands and feet get cold, even if they are well insulated. Good circulation will not be restored to them until the body core warms up. This is why putting on extra mittens and socks doesn't warm your extremities as long as your body is chilled. The circulation to them is still kept at a minimal level. If you get cold enough, your body will totally shut down circulation to the extremities in order to preserve the essential core temperature—sacrificing the limbs for survival. Freezing of the hands and feet can then occur, with consequent frostbite. Serious frostbite occurring in natural circumstances nearly always follows hypothermia.

Runners generate a lot of heat when they are moving well, and the only real danger of hypothermia results from misjudgment of your own capabilities or the weather conditions. Such mistakes are easy to make, however, especially if you have not done much cold-weather running before. Though the danger of cold weather is much less than that of heat, running in snow, ice, and cold often requires quite high expenditures of energy. The runner may tire earlier than usual on a long run.

Stormy weather coming up in the middle of a long run can radically change conditions, particularly if you find you have to fight a cold head wind all the way home. In addition, normal fatigue in the later stages of a run has quite different consequences in cold weather, because your heat production drops, reserves are very low, and your clothes may be wet from perspiration, condensation of your breath, and precipitation. These problems are all compounded if a storm comes in during your run. Winter storms commonly bring with them sudden temperature drops of thirty degrees or more Fahrenheit, accompanied by wind and precipitation.

The point at which you begin to slow radically—known as "the wall" in long races—is not uncommon during extended training runs, when it is not usually particularly painful or stressful, because you respond by simply reducing your pace to a jog. The slowing is indicative of the exhaustion of glycogen reserves in the leg muscles and often a lowered blood sugar. During training, such depletion often occurs quite a bit sooner than it would in a race, because the training schedule is not as likely to be designed to allow the muscles and liver to completely rebuild their stores. Any extra energy demands imposed by the weather will cause depletion to occur even sooner.

The danger in winter arises from the greatly lowered capacity for heat production that accompanies depletion. If you are out on a twenty-mile circuit from your house, swinging comfortably along at seven-minute miles, and you hit the wall at thirteen miles, you still have seven miles to go before you get home. At this point you are likely to have slowed to a nine-minute pace with greatly reduced heat production, because you must now rely on the much slower metabolism of fat to supply your energy. All these problems are likely to be compounded by cooling temperatures, wet clothing, and stiffening muscles slowing you down still more.

To run safely in the cold, you should avoid taking routes far from home until you have a good feeling for the demands of cold-weather running and the variations in weather patterns along your routes. Be particularly careful about running in areas where there is little traffic and few houses, normally the best places to run. Pay close attention to the normal storm and wind patterns where you live. Running back against the wind will slow you and require a lot more energy even if you still have plenty of reserves, and the wind-chill factor can rob your body of a great deal of heat at the same time. You may be perfectly warm with a sweater in still air but desperately cold without a Windbreaker when a breeze comes up.

Because of these potential difficulties, you should be careful to carry enough warm clothing to handle contingencies when you go for long runs in the winter. Tie a sweater and windbreaker around your waist, or tuck a hat and wind-pants in the pocket of your warm-up jacket. The exact clothing you carry will depend on the weather, your own metabolism, the distance of the run, and so on. You have to judge from your own experience. The important point is that runners who are moving at full speed dress very lightly for the weather and can cover a lot of ground. Turning an ankle ten miles out on a country road with the snow swirling around can quickly turn a pleasant and easy run into a survival ordeal. A little advance thought about your clothing and a little care in learning your capacities can prevent some very unpleasant experiences.

Your clothing needn't be fancy or expensive. Sweaters and

nylon shells too battered for other uses are just as effective as fancy running suits. Wearing several layers of clothing allows you to adjust your insulation to suit your needs. Lightweight, windproof shell clothing is often more useful than heavy insulated jackets, because a shell allows you to dissipate a lot of heat yet does not permit much wind penetration or absorb much moisture. It weighs very little but guards against the most significant change in conditions, a rise in the wind when you are many miles from home. A light wool sweater underneath will usually keep you warm. If you don't have some suitable old clothes at home and don't want to spend a lot of money, you should be able to outfit yourself in style at the nearest Salvation Army store.

Don't neglect protection for your head and hands when you are running in the cold. Your hands will often become chilled when you are running, because they are exposed to the cold but aren't doing very much. The blood supply is directed mainly to the working muscles of your legs, especially on a long and strenuous run. A lot of runners use old socks to keep their hands warm. All the digits are next to each other so that they stay warmer, and manual dexterity is not much needed during running.

A hat is by far the most useful single item of clothing, apart from those items required to avoid arrest for indecent exposure. Because of the concentration of vital organs in the head, circulation there remains good even when the body is shutting down the blood supply to the hands and feet. Because of its large surface area and excellent blood supply, the head and neck can radiate tremendous amounts of heat. It thus provides one of the best places to add and subtract insulation for heat regulation, particularly since a hat is one of the easiest pieces of clothing to don and remove. When you get cold, pull on your hat, and when you start to overheat, take it off. A high collar, a long hat, a scarf, or some combination that can be used to cover the neck is also helpful.

Treatment for Hypothermia

The signs of hypothermia are irrationality, stumbling, slurred speech, bluish coloring around the nails, lips, and mucous membranes, irritability, and lack of motivation. The victim is typically unaware of what is going on, unless a lot of experience with cold-weather activities has made him alert to the effects of cold. If you notice any of these signs in a running companion or yourself, it is important to get to the nearest source of warmth, whether it is a passing car or a roadside house. A hypothermia victim is likely to claim to be fine and object to your concern, but deterioration can be rapid and dangerous. Even if home is only a mile or so away, don't let someone who seems to be suffering from hypothermia go on if help is available.

Once you have gotten a victim or yourself out of the cold, first aid depends on the circumstances and severity of the problem. Rewarming is vital, and it is important to realize that if the victim is very cold and apparently in something of a stupor, his body may have become incapable of bringing itself back up to its proper temperature. In such cases all available outside sources of heat should be used to provide warmth until the victim has returned to normal. Severe cases should receive medical attention if it is available, since shock may result when the cold blood at the extremities is released and returns to the heat. Unless medical help is immediately available, however, warming the victim is still the safest possibility. A warm bath is ideal; electric blankets, heating pads, or other people snuggling in blankets with the affected person are all good alternatives. Hot drinks are helpful for those able to drink them.

Frostbite and Frostnip

Deep frostbite—of the kind that requires hospitalization and may result in the loss of fingers or toes—is not a serious danger for runners. It might occur only if someone suffered a serious case of hypothermia and spent a long period exposed to the cold in an unconscious or semiconscious state. One can conceive of circumstances in which this might happen, but it is quite unlikely.

Frostnip is not a technical term, but it has quite a clear meaning and is far more likely among runners. Serious chilling of an extremity, perhaps with some surface freezing, can result in an injury very like a burn. There is second-stage blistering, a good deal of stinging pain, and a subsequent peeling-off of several layers of skin.

Cold injuries to the extremities occur in two ways. The first is simply exposure of the skin to extreme cold for some period. This is most commonly due to cold wind, perhaps combined with blowing snow. It is a particular hazard to the ears and the face, especially the nose. Freezing of these parts and the flesh over the cheekbones can easily affect a runner moving into a cold wind, especially in blizzard conditions. It is not usually really serious, because the good circulation to the rest of the head generally prevents deep freezing, so that extensive tissue damage is unlikely. The consequences are still quite painful, however, and are likely to result in long-term sensitivity of the affected areas to the cold.

The remedy is to protect your face with a mask, a ski hat, a scarf, or something else, so that the wind can't chill it excessively. Checking your face and ears occasionally with your hands can be important in avoiding frostnip. Once an ear or nose becomes numb, you will not notice when it starts to freeze. Thus if your face feels uncomfortably cold and then stops bothering you, it is usually a sign that it is becoming dangerously cold. Stop a minute and warm it, unless you are having other more serious problems. If your nose or ear feels very cold when you touch it with your hands, you are starting to suffer frostnip. After rewarming, either with your hands or in a warm room, a frostnipped area will begin to sting and burn. Try to avoid rubbing with your hands, which will only damage more tissue. The damage caused by frostnip will be much like that of a superficial burn.

The other mechanism for cold injury is through a combination of cold and reduced circulation. It can be caused by tight shoes or by the mechanism described in connection with hypothermia. If your body becomes badly chilled, circulation to the extremities will be reduced. Naturally, a number of factors can work together. If your shoes are too tight, you've become chilled, your socks become wet, and there is a cold wind blowing, you have a better chance of suffering some cold injury to your feet than if only one of these factors is present. Slight freezing of the fingertips or the tips of the toes will produce the same sensations on thawing as frostnip of the face, though blistering and pain in these areas will be more serious. If serious swelling and blistering occurs from any cold injury, or if deep freezing is evident, seek medical help.

The best sign of incipient frostbite in any area is whiteness. If you are running with a companion in cold weather, check each other's faces occasionally, and stop to warm them if any white areas begin to show. Toes and fingers should be checked and warmed if they become numb after being painfully cold. Any real frostbite, indicated by a part of the body that is white and hard, should receive medical attention at the earliest possible time. *Never* rub such tissue; if medical attention cannot be obtained right away, the tissue should be thawed in very warm (not hot) water and protected from any chafing or rubbing until medical care is obtained. Such tissue can always be saved, but it must be treated with great care. The thawing is quite painful.

Unless it results from some freak accident, frostbite is a completely preventable injury. With reasonable care in keeping warm, not getting too far afield in cold weather, and protecting bare skin from cold wind, you should never have a problem with hypothermia or frostbite.

Special Cautions for Men

Running into a cold wind with warm-up pants that are not completely windproof can result in painful cold injuries to the genitals. This is not usually noticed until you get home, after the damage is done. Any windproof barrier will prevent the difficulty. Some runners wear regular running shorts over long johns or warm-up pants, while others wear something underneath. A layer of nylon can be sewn inside the front of the pants. Not all pants allow enough wind through to cause a problem, but you should be careful when you start running with a new combination of clothes.

Breathing Cold Air

You cannot freeze your lungs by running in the cold, though this is an oft-repeated myth. Inhaling in extreme cold is sometimes rather shocking, and it is easy to understand why people might fear the possibility of freezing. But the air is warmed as it is inhaled, before it reaches the tiny airways of the lungs, no matter how hard you are breathing. In very cold weather, however, there can be other problems associated with breathing cold air.

The drying effect of cold air has already been mentioned. People who are having trouble with respiratory infections should probably stop running altogether in cold weather. Those who are especially prone to colds or flu in winter may want to try to run at an indoor track or to substitute some other form of cardiovascular exercise, at least on the coldest days. But most runners will have no difficulty training outside through the cold months. I love to run during cold weather. There is an especially exhilarating feeling about running over squeaky-cold snow before dawn, under the crisp winter stars.

One thing that breathing very cold air definitely can do is cool your body. When you are breathing hard, the chilling effect can be substantial. If you are cold, it is usually best to run at a fairly comfortable aerobic pace, so that your breathing does not become labored. Save your speed bursts for a time during the run when you feel reasonably warm.

A few people are actually allergic to cold and have strong unpleasant reactions to it. If you are plagued with this trouble, you will simply have to find through experimentation whether any clothing adjustments will permit you to run.

All the minor troubles of running in the cold may be alleviated by use of a ski mask, scarf, or similar device. Molded foam masks, which warm and moisten incoming air slightly, are available specifically for those who have trouble breathing cold air. They present relatively little resistance to breathing. They are similar to the dust masks made for carpenters and others working in areas where the air contains a lot of particulate matter. They are washable and reusable. Wearers of glasses, who already have constant fogging problems in cold weather, will find that all of these devices make fogging worse.

Bursitis

Another difficulty that can be associated with cold-weather running is bursitis, which is sometimes precipitated by chilling. The bursae are liquid-filled sacs that act as cushions in some of the joints. Bursitis is an inflammation of one of the bursae, a condition that we have discussed elsewhere. Cold-weather running can precipitate bursitis of the shoulder in susceptible individuals if the upper body becomes chilled. The remedy is simply to make sure you keep warm. Be particularly careful if you have had bursitis before. The condition is unpleasant but not serious, and it will eventually disappear, usually in a week or two.

CHAPTER 16

Heat Injuries

H OT WEATHER may lack some of the dramatic aura of the
cold, perhaps because frostbite is an unfamiliar threat
with a hint of mystery about it. The potential danger of being
caught out in severe cold with inadequate clothing is clear
enough to make us shiver at the prospect. On a hot day we
know that little clothing is needed except to prevent sunburn.
The dangers of heat are insidious, but they are far more
threatening to the runner than cold. Dehydration, heat exhaustion, and heat stroke can threaten any runner, not just
the careless person who goes out wholly unprepared, like a
potential hypothermia victim in winter. They stalk even the
best runners during races in high temperatures and humidity,
and they can strike quickly, sometimes fatally.

The body has no defense in hot weather comparable to the

ones it can use in cold weather, when the act of running itself provides some protection, producing large quantities of heat as long as the runner retains sufficient energy reserves. In hot weather the exercise and the temperature are working together to defeat the body's cooling mechanisms. If high humidity is added, too, the combination can be overwhelming. If you doubt this, look at the effect on racing times in long-distance races. At Boston, for example, the fastest time ever run in a United States marathon was recorded by Bill Rodgers in 1975—2:09:55. The hot and humid race of the following year was won by Jack Fultz in 2:20:19. 1977 was also hot, though not quite as bad as 1976, and Jerome Drayton won the race in 2:14:46. Rodgers, one of the greatest marathoners the United States has ever produced and a native of the Boston area, was forced out of the race both years by the heat. 1978 brought cool weather for the race, and Rodgers led the pack once again with a 2:10:13. Fultz ran nine minutes faster than his 1976 winning time, but this year it was only good for fourth. The difference made by the heat and humidity is enormous.

The effects on less well-trained runners is even greater. The contestants at Boston are far more experienced and better conditioned than those in the average marathon, because most of the official entrants have to meet special qualifying standards. Men under forty must have run a marathon during the previous year in less than three hours, and there is a time limit of three and one half hours for women and older men. Yet even with an elite field, an appalling number of people in 1976 and 1977 dropped out of the race suffering badly from the heat, or finished in a condition of near-collapse.

In long-distance racing, especially at the length of the marathon or more, dehydration becomes one of the major limiting factors on performance, even in mild temperatures. During really hot weather it is likely to become the single most important element for the runner.

Quite apart from the dangers of severe heat injury—primarily heat stroke—the aftereffects of stressing the body beyond its capacities in hot weather can last for some time, interfering with training progress and with normal running. Other injuries may be sustained if you try to ignore the additional load that heat imposes on your body and continue a normal training load. After the dehydration of a severely stressful hot-weather run, your leg muscles may be sore for days, and the general level of your body's reserves is bound to be considerably lowered.

How the Body Deals with Heat

Many of the organs of the body are even more sensitive to heat than to cold. Vital functions deteriorate rather quickly if the temperature of the body core drops, and the victim of hypothermia may not recuperate once body temperature has fallen ten degrees Fahrenheit. Still, with proper treatment victims have recovered without significant permanent damage despite much lower body temperatures. The body is far less tolerant of excess heat. A ten-degree rise in temperature may cause permanent brain damage—if the victim survives.

When the body starts to overheat, its first reaction is to increase circulation to the skin and the extremities, so that the warm blood can lose heat to the environment, like the water pumped through a car's radiator. In order to cool the skin so that more heat can be lost, sweating also takes place. A great deal of heat is required to change water from a liquid to a vapor, and much of this heat will be drawn from the skin and the warm blood near its surface. This cooling mechanism is much less effective when the humidity is high and the air is already nearly saturated with water vapor.

Sweating seems particularly profuse when the atmosphere

is humid, because the perspiration runs off your skin but little evaporation actually takes place. A light wind from behind you also interferes with evaporation and cooling, because it effectively neutralizes your forward motion through the air.

The blood circulation to the skin that is required to cool the body imposes an additional load on the circulatory system of a runner, who requires a good blood supply to the working muscles. In normal circumstances the additional work causes no real problem for the well-trained athlete, but for beginners who may have some weakness in their hearts it is an important consideration. Heart attack is possible and heat stroke far more likely for such individuals, particularly if they are overweight.

Extra body fat makes dissipation of excess heat far more difficult. The muscles are doing more work to push the body along, generating more heat. At the same time, getting rid of the heat is harder for two reasons. First, the layer of fat near the skin is a good insulator; that is why marine mammals that swim in cold water have a thick layer. Second, you can get rid of heat better the more surface area you have for a given body weight. Thinner people have more surface area for their weight.

The amount of liquid used for cooling by perspiration is an important factor in hot-weather running. The fluid reserves of the body are obviously limited, and the amount of liquid that can be spared without affecting performance is smaller still. If the liquid is obtained from the blood, the loss of very much volume will begin to affect the circulatory system. Runners who have properly acclimatized to heat and who are well trained obtain much of the fluid used for sweating from muscle tissue rather than from the blood, so they do not suffer circulatory collapse after sustaining weight losses from perspiration that would be dangerous for the average individual. This loss of liquid still has severe imbalancing effects on body chemistry, however. The concentrations of soluble substances within the cells are changed when water is lost, and this causes severe disruptions of normal function.

It is an obvious inference from these effects of dehydration that the distance runner should use every possible technique to dissipate heat, especially during distance races, and to supply the body with as much water as it can absorb. It is not possible for a runner functioning at a high level of effort in hot weather to absorb liquids from the stomach as fast as they are used, but a significant amount can be taken in. The runner should drink often during hot weather running. As well as supplying extra liquid, cold drinks absorb heat in the process of being brought up to body temperature. Small drinks taken frequently supply the necessary fluid without causing discomfort.

It is important to note that in addition to factors like weight and acclimatization, there is a good deal of variation between individuals in their tolerance to heat and their ability to dissipate it. You can improve both your safety and performance in hot weather by carefully preparing for hot-weather running, but you also have to accept your individual limitations. Among world-class runners, for example, some individuals consistently do well in hot-weather races, while others usually do rather poorly. Bill Rodgers generally fades in a marathon with hot, humid weather. Frank Shorter likes hot-weather marathons, because he is less affected by the heat than many other top racers. Acclimatization will enable you to run more safely in hot weather and approach your own potential, but it does not bring equal hot-weather capacity to all.

Heat Acclimatization

The most important factor in dealing with heat is good

sense. There is no substitute for the realization that heat imposes significant stress on any runner's body. During hot, humid weather you should run during the cooler parts of the day if you can, except when acclimatizing. Drinking during your training runs helps to prevent chronic dehydration. Finally, good judgment in races and hard training runs is crucial, because of the threat of heat injuries and severe overstress when running in the heat. Losing any extra weight is probably the best single measure you can take to prepare for hot-weather running if you are carrying any significant amount of fat.

Besides these precautions, training the body to deal with hot weather is important if you plan to do any distance racing in the heat. A runner who is used to running in the heat will be far better able to cope with high temperatures and humidity than one who has done all of his recent training in cool weather. Preparation is both psychological and physical. Distance racing is always as much a mental discipline as a physical one, and much depends on the runner's ability to judge the body's reserves and capacity. Recent running in the heat is the best mental preparation both for the discomfort involved and for accurate assessment of one's capabilities matched against the conditions.

Physical adjustments of the acclimatized runner probably include a number of changes that are not completely understood, but several of them have been well documented. Perspiration increases, but the loss of electrolytes in the sweat is reduced. (Electrolytes are compounds that are soluble in water, producing ions that will conduct electrical current through the cells. Common salt is an example.) The ability of the heat-acclimatized body to cool itself is much greater, and the runner will be more comfortable, have a lower heart rate, a lower body temperature, and less fatigue than a person who has not run recently in hot conditions.

Like other forms of acclimatization, the ability to tolerate heat is gained or lost with exposure or lack of it. If you plan to run in a distance race in possible heat, you should train in the heat for at least a few weeks in advance. The simplest way to accomplish this is to run in the heat two or three days a week. If you don't feel uncomfortably warm and don't perspire a good deal, you probably aren't acclimatizing much. Runners who are training in a cool region for a hot-weather race can simulate most of the conditions of sweltering heat simply by wearing a lot of clothing. A couple of hot runs a week for six weeks should thoroughly acclimatize you to running in the heat.

Some runners, particularly Tom Osler, have found that eliminating table salt from the diet is a great help in dealing with heat. There is no doubt that enough salt to fulfill the body's requirements can be obtained from a normal diet without the addition of salt in cooking or at the table. Many foods contain some salt in their natural state. It is also clear that the heat cramps sometimes associated with inadequate salt are in fact due to lack of acclimatization. Whether elimination of added salt from the diet will improve most runners' tolerance to heat, however, is still a matter of debate.

Clothing

Proper choice of clothing can reduce the effects of heat, particularly in direct sun. The body absorbs a lot of the sun's rays, so bright sun will add significantly to the heat stress on the runner. Light-colored clothing that will reflect sunlight is a definite help if it is also porous, so that it does not interfere with heat loss from perspiration. Many runners will find that a suitable light-colored hat with a sun visor will help, too. It should be well ventilated. Clothing also provides useful protection from sunburn.

Remember that the function of a shirt and hat for hot-

weather running is to reflect the sun without interfering with
the body's cooling mechanism. A tightly woven nylon shirt
in a dark color will make you hotter, not cooler. Mesh and
net materials are good for allowing air to get through while
still shading your skin. Mesh is particularly good around the
midriff, where much of the body's cooling takes place.

Glare can cause headaches as well as eye discomfort. If
you wear glasses, prescription sunglasses are a help. Those
who don't have to wear glasses may prefer to use an eyeshade
or a hat with a visor to reduce glare, rather than sunglasses.

Drinking

During hot-weather distance running, fluid replacement
can be important for safety. For most runners it also helps
improve performance, though top-level marathoners can finish a hot-weather race in good time without drinking. The
best strategy seems to be to take a large drink shortly before
beginning a hot-weather run. Drinking too long before will
result in the extra liquid being excreted as urine. A pint of
water five minutes before a race is probably about right.
Small drinks should be taken frequently during the run.

Many runners like to use electrolyte replacement drinks,
either a commercially made variety or a personal formula.
ERG, Gatorade, and Body Punch are common brands.
These drinks are designed to replace electrolytes lost in sweating. They may be of some use, but electrolytes can also be
replaced fairly easily after the run. Fluid replacement is of
prime importance during the run. Sugar in any form, including honey, will slow the emptying of the stomach in large
concentrations, so it is better to drink either plain water or
diluted electrolyte-replacement drinks or juices. Sugar concentration should not exceed 25 grams per liter (2.5 percent
by weight) or it will slow your uptake of the liquid in your
stomach. Most commercial drinks are 5 to 10 percent sugar,

so it is probably wise to dilute them by half. A practical way to do this during a race is to alternate between water and commercial preparations at aid stations.

Heat Stroke

Heat stroke is a potentially fatal form of heat injury. It is fortunately uncommon among trained runners, but it is a true medical emergency and must receive immediate first aid when it occurs.

Heat stroke results from a complete breakdown of the body's cooling system. The victim stops sweating, probably because of an overload of the circulatory system, and the temperature of the body starts to rise catastrophically. The symptoms are easily recognized. The victim's skin becomes flushed, dry, and hot. The temperature of the whole body is obviously very hot, and the person appears to have a fever and to be very ill. The victim may lose consciousness.

First aid is also straightforward. The victim must be cooled off immediately by any available means, preferably by pouring cool liquid on the body. Do not delay treatment in case of heat stroke. Get the victim into the shade, and pour any liquids that can be obtained on the skin, hose the person down, or rub the body with ice. Massage the extremities during cooling to help get the cooled blood back to the body core. Fanning may be useful if no liquids are available. Drinks are of little use in the case of heat stroke. Once the person has been cooled down, avoid excessive chilling, and watch for possible recurrence of the syndrome. A victim of heat stroke should receive medical attention as soon as possible. His temperature may remain unstable for several days.

Victims of heat stroke should be helped to lie down, but *never* covered with blankets or other insulation, which will trap heat and worsen their condition. Remember that the problem is caused by excessive buildup of heat, and that treatment must always be aimed at cooling the victim off.

Heat Exhaustion

Heat exhaustion is fairly common in hot weather races and runs. It is far less serious than stroke, though heat stroke may sometimes follow heat exhaustion. Heat exhaustion is similar to fainting or shock in its symptoms and immediate causes. In its attempt to maintain circulation to the skin so that there will be adequate cooling, the body loses adequate pressure in the circulatory system, and the brain doesn't get enough blood. The victim is likely to show signs of dizziness, to stagger, and perhaps to faint. The skin is pale and damp, and temperature is approximately normal. The skin may even seem cool.

The victim of heat exhaustion should lie down in the shade, feet slightly elevated, and should be kept comfortable and given drinks when he is conscious enough to swallow them. If you are affected, lie down before you fall down. If you see someone else suffering from heat exhaustion, try to persuade the person to lie down and drink something. The affected person should not get up until he's had a chance to recover and absorb some liquid. The victim is likely to feel fine after lying down, since an adequate blood supply to the brain is restored by the position. But the racer who tries to start off again is likely to collapse.

Other Difficulties

Heat cramps are primarily a result of the loss of too much salt during heavy exercise. Salty drinks and stretching the effected muscles should cure the cramps. As suggested earlier in the chapter, however, these cramps are usually *caused* by inadequate acclimatization to heat. Extra salt should not be needed by properly trained runners, who will not lose as much salt during exercise. The body does build up a tolerance for large quantities of salt, and those who are used to large quantities may be more subject to heat cramps than others. If you plan to reduce salt intake during hot weather, do it gradually, so that the body has time to adjust.

Sunburn is caused by excessive exposure to ultraviolet radiation from the sun. It is not a major problem for most runners, since regular exposure gives some protection. Upright posture keeps most parts of the runner's body from receiving too much sun, and training runs are usually shorter than sunbathing sessions on the beach. Some people are a lot more sensitive to the sun than others, however, and those with pale complexions may need to be careful, especially in the spring. Using a shirt and a sun visor will usually prevent burns until you have built up a tan. If your hair is thin, you may need a hat. Screening lotions work only until they are washed off by perspiration, so they are of little help to runners training in hot weather.

Chronic dehydration can be a significant problem for those doing hard training in hot weather. Runners frequently aren't thirsty enough to replace all the liquid lost in sweating. This seems to be partly a matter of individual body chemistry and partly one of habit, but it is fairly common. Part of the problem is simply that huge amounts of liquid can be lost each day while you're running long distances in hot weather.

A loss of ten pounds at the end of a run is fairly common, and in this case you have to drink five quarts of liquid just to replace the water lost in perspiration, in addition to normal needs. The primary signs of chronic dehydration are weight loss and amber-colored urine that persists into the evening or the morning after a run. Many people have to consciously drink as much liquid as they can comfortably manage to stay adequately hydrated during hot-weather training.

Part IV

INJURIES THAT BEGIN WITH THE FEET

CHAPTER 17

The Running Body

SOME COMPREHENSION of the overall movement of the body during running is helpful in understanding the development of overuse injuries. The most recalcitrant overuse injuries are the ones due to stresses created by the way the body moves while running. Differences in the ways our bodies are constructed bring excessive stress to bear on parts of the legs and feet of some runners. In the highly demanding activity of running, these structures may start to break down. Clearly, the harder you train, the closer you will approach the limits that all of the joints, tendons, and muscles of your legs and feet can stand. If a few areas are already being overworked because of structural imbalances, they are quite likely to collapse under the pressure of hard training.

If excessive motion of your feet is placing a lot of unnecessary torque on your knees, an increase in your training load may precipitate problems that would not have appeared if you had progressed more slowly. On the other hand, they might also have been prevented by using foot supports, even without reducing the training load. The combination is what causes the injury. Someone with a more serious problem or someone under other kinds of stress might have to have both foot supports *and* a lower level of training to prevent injury. Because the factors affect one another, no magic formula exists to distinguish their influences. You have to be aware of both.

The importance of avoiding too much stress has been emphasized repeatedly in this book. This chapter and the following one deal mainly with mechanical imbalances in the body. It is important to keep the relationship between the factors in mind, however. Even if you are working with a podiatrist, you have to remember that your training program will have as much influence on your recovery or continued health as will any mechanical supports the doctor may devise. A good podiatrist will be able to tell far more about the effects of mechanical imbalances than you can, but you know far more about your training and the way your body reacts to it. Don't fall into the trap of assuming that foot supports will prevent all running injuries or of relying on the doctor for all evaluations. The best that supports can do is to balance the stresses on your legs and feet so that no single structure is receiving more of the load than the rest of the legs. Too much work will still cause a breakdown.

How the Runner Moves

Even many experienced distance runners tend to retain some of the image of the moving body that is typical in our culture—that of the sprinter moving off the blocks, leaning far forward, the feet driving from behind, with the running done from the balls of the feet. This is not what you see if you study the movements of distance runners, however, or even those of middle-distance specialists. The body is generally upright and relaxed. Look at the pictures of Frank Shorter, Bill Rodgers, and other accomplished distance runners, not only while they're running marathons but during much shorter races. You will see upright torsos, heads level and facing straight ahead, and moderate arm motion. Feet usually hit the ground heel-first, rolling down to absorb impact with the whole foot before becoming rigid for the push-off. The center of gravity of the body moves up and down very little and doesn't rock from side to side. The closer it approximates moving forward in a straight line, the less waste motion there is.

Running is a series of coordinated jumps. The runner takes off from one foot, is completely airborne during an intermediate phase, and then lands on the other foot, moving forward then for another jump. The exaggerated motions required for attaining any height or for increasing distance are all eliminated, however, since the runner wants to do as little work against gravity as possible.

We are not concerned with technique as applied to winning races here, so the question of improving efficiency is not important. Note that good runners usually use a relatively fast, compact stride, however. Overstriding is hard on the legs, but it is ineffective as well. The oft-repeated advice to "lengthen your stride" does not really improve your running. As the pace increases, the actual ground gained with each step increases, but not through the mechanism of reaching out forward with the feet.

Learning to run with your feet meeting the ground gently

is often a good way to improve efficiency and reduce the stress on your legs. We should note, though, that style flows from individual physiology as well as from training. An odd movement of your arm may be a natural way of balancing a quirk in the structure of the opposite leg.

The actual movements of the runner's body are important as a prelude to our consideration of the feet. When you stand in a normal position, the center of gravity of your body is centered between your feet. (The center of gravity is the balance point of your body. If you could be hung from a string attached to the center of gravity, you would be stable in any position—the weight on either side would balance the weight on the other. In many analyses of motion it is possible to treat a whole body as if it were a weight concentrated at its center of gravity. Your center of gravity in a running position is in your abdomen.)

When you walk, you place a foot on one side of the line along which you're traveling. The other foot is then placed on the other side of the line as you step forward. You actually shift your center of gravity back and forth across the line, moving it over each foot in turn. When you're running, though, your feet fall much more closely to being directly under the middle of your body. They hit almost along the line you are following in your forward motion. On an average, the inside edges of your feet will just touch that line as you run straight forward. Your center of gravity scarcely sways back and forth at all.

The motion of the body during running is interesting. The pelvis swings with each forward step, rotating somewhat to allow the leading leg to swing forward and the trailing one to move back. This pelvic rotation is much more accentuated than it is in normal walking. To balance the motion of the legs, the arms swing back and forth in opposite sequence from the legs, and the shoulders rotate counter to the rotation of the pelvis. Neither of these motions is exaggerated in good runners, especially in distance running, but it is very definite. Note the actions of the runner in the drawing, which represents a rather fast pace. The runner drives off the ball of the foot while driving the opposite arm forward. There is then a phase in which both feet are off the ground, and the leading foot reaches forward to cushion its contact with the ground. The foot does not actually hit the ground much ahead of the runner's center of gravity, though.

The foot strike is one of the important factors in all analysis of overuse injuries. It will be considered in detail in the next chapter, but it should be mentioned here. Note that the runner in the illustration lands on the outside of his heel first, rolls down onto the rest of the foot, and finally takes off from the ball. The great majority of distance runners and many runners at shorter distances use this action, which cushions the landing. Most really good competitors in a 10,000-meter race land this way, and they are running at roughly a 4½-minute-per-mile pace. Some runners land with the entire outside edge of the foot at the same time, rolling to the inside. Landing with the ball of the foot first usually occurs only in sprinting, and it provides far less cushioning than a heel-first landing. The details of the motion of the foot while it is on the ground will be discussed in the next chapter.

One other point worth noting in the side view of the runner in the illustration is the action of the knee. Most people think of the knee as exerting a major part of the forward force of the stride. An examination of the illustration will show that there is far less motion during the propulsive phase than most people think. The knee extends slightly as the runner pushes off, but not much. Really accentuated knee action

a   b   c   d

A typical distance runner moving at a fast pace, showing the motion of the body during running. At a the runner is just pushing off from his left foot and is driving forward with the left arm. At this point the foot has to be acting as a rigid lever to permit a straight forward push. Note that the pelvis is turned so that the right side is forward; the shoulders are angled in the reverse direction. The head faces straight ahead. In b the runner is airborne, using his forward momentum to carry him to the next landing. His arm is crossing the body a little too much, wasting energy. In c the right foot is about to land, and the front muscles of the lower leg have pulled the toes up in preparation for the landing. The left leg is starting to bend to swing forward, and the right arm is beginning its forward swing. In

e   f   g   h

d *the right foot has begun to land, and the whole leg is starting to rotate inward on the hip joint. As we will see in the next chapter, the foot is beginning to* pronate, *or roll inward. Note that the left leg is bent, forming a short pendulum that will swing forward rapidly. In* e *the landing phase is complete. The shoulders and hips are square, and the foot will now begin to* supinate, *or roll outward, so that it can become a rigid lever. At* f *the right heel is leaving the ground and the arm is moving forward rapidly. This is the position of the body occurring just before* a, *except with the opposite leg. In* g *we see the runner just following takeoff, comparable to a phase just before* b. *In* h *the runner is about to land on his left foot.*

occurs when the leg is brought forward, and this is seen mainly in runners who are moving at a fast pace. It is done because a pendulum or swinging object with a certain weight and pushing force will move forward much faster if it is shorter. The leg moving forward is a pendulum, and by bending the knee the runner shortens the pendulum and speeds up the forward movement.

The Legs

The motions of the legs are primary in running, of course, and some understanding of them is critical to the understanding of the effects of the structure of the feet. The basic structure and muscle groups in the legs are shown in the illustrations on pages 89 and 98. The underlying skeletal structure and the way that it can be moved is critical.

Remember that the bones are essentially rigid, though they are made up of living tissue that responds to stress like the other parts of the body. The ends of the bones are shaped in various ways so that they will fit together in *joints*. The joints can be constructed to allow anything from a very wide range of motion to hardly any at all. Cartilage, fluid-excreting enclosures, and other specialized cushioning and lubricating methods are used to smooth the movement of the joints. The joints are surrounded by inelastic *ligaments*—strong, fibrous tissue designed to prevent excessive movement of the joints when they are overstressed. The joints of the legs are constructed so that they are normally held in place by the weight of the body, and the ligaments generally come into play only when the joint is stressed in an unusual way.

Because the body is built on a rather rigid frame in order to withstand the force of gravity, most of it is supported by the bones, and all the movements involving the weight of the body as a whole take place through movement at the joints.

(In parts of the body where major weight is not borne, like the face and the mouth, less rigid and more plastic cartilage can be used to provide basic support.) *Muscles* are attached on either side of the joints to move them in various directions. Muscles can exert force only by contracting.

Remember that some muscles attach directly to bone, but most attach through tendons, relatively inelastic fibrous tissue similar to ligaments, except that tendons attach muscle to bone, while ligaments attach bone to bone. One similarity that has great importance for runners is the poor circulation and slow healing capacity in both tendons and ligaments.

The *hip joint* is the only one in the leg with true freedom of motion in three dimensions. It is a ball-and-socket joint, while the other joints in both the leg and the foot are far more limited in motion. The *ankle joint* seems at first glance to have similar, though less extensive, freedom; but actually some of this motion comes from the foot joint below the anklebone, some from the relative movement of the two bones in the lower leg, and some all the way down from the hip.

It is important to note that the *femur,* or *thighbone,* descends at an angle from the hip rather than straight down, especially when you are running. This has to be true, since the two hip joints are the width of the pelvis apart, and yet the feet hit the ground during running in an almost straight line. The lower legs are normally fairly straight, which means that there is some sideways stress in the knees due to the angle of the femur as it enters the knee joint. Women have wider pelvises to allow for childbirth, so their femurs enter both the pelvis and the knees at sharper angles than in men. This provides a ready explanation for the somewhat greater vulnerability to knee injury that some authorities have found in women.

Variations in the angle of the femur and the knees—bowlegs, knock-knees, and similar anatomical variations—can stress the knees in unusual ways, causing chronic weaknesses. Similar problems occur if one leg is significantly shorter than the other, a difference that is very hard to see unless the variation is quite large.

The basic structure of the leg and foot proceeds down from the hip joint. Remember that the pelvis turns in the direction of forward motion while you are running. In order to keep the foot, the knee joint, and the ankle joint pointed roughly forward as you run, *the femur has to turn on its own axis,* using the hip joint for the freedom of rotation. Thus as you swing your leg forward in midstride, the whole leg is actually turning outward, away from the body. After the foot comes into contact with the ground, the leg rotates back inward, compensating for the pelvis moving the other way. This rotational movement of the leg is very important, but it is something we are not instinctively aware of. It has important consequences, because the knee and ankle joints allow only straight forward-and-back motion, so the compensation for this rotation at the other end of the limb all takes place in the foot, along with cushioning of the impact of foot strike and any necessary adjustments for uneven ground. There must be some accommodation for the rotation back and forth of the leg, because during the time that the foot is actually in contact with the ground, the sole of the shoe is fixed in position. It is also clear that if the rotational movements of the femur and foot are not properly coordinated, there will be a good deal of stress on the leg and joints between.

Before proceeding on to other details of the leg, we should review the major muscle groups. (See the illustrations on pages 89 and 98.) The *hamstrings,* the main group of muscles at the back of the thigh, help to drive the leg backward and exert all the force to bend the knee. Along with the calf muscles, they are the major propulsive muscles in distance running. The *quadriceps* are the muscles at the front of the thigh that extend the knee. The muscles at the back of the *calf* extend the foot and thus provide much of the driving force in running. They operate through the *Achilles tendon*, which attaches to the heel. The muscle at the outer front of the calf, the *front tibial muscle (anterior tibialis)*, and the *rear tibial muscle (posterior tibialis)*, which is hidden behind the shinbone, both act to raise the inner border of the foot and help to support the arch. The front tibial muscle also helps to raise the front of the foot on the ankle joint. These two muscles and their tendons are the ones involved in shinsplints. Finally, the *muscles of the groin* are used to pull the whole leg inward toward the center of the pelvis and are sometimes pulled during hard running.

The Knee

The most vulnerable part of the leg should be considered in detail before we go on to the foot, partly because it is so often injured as a result of distortion of the foot. The knee is an extremely important joint, as everyone who injures one finds out. It is the largest joint in the body and one that is hard to understand at first because of the complicating feature of the kneecap.

The knee is not a true hinge joint like the elbow, but it acts like one. When functioning properly it will permit only backward and forward motion of the lower leg, and the joint will not bend forward. Side-to-side motion is prevented because the basic knee joint is a double one. There are two ball joints side by side, so that only single-plane motion can occur. The femur—the thighbone—has two large balls on the bottom end, which ride in two sockets at the top of the

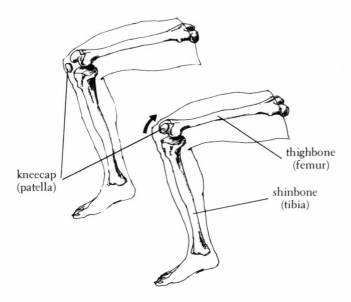

The action of the kneecap. The kneecap is not tightly bound to the joint. It acts like a pulley for the quadriceps—*the front thigh muscles. The quadriceps are attached to the top of the kneecap; the bottom of the kneecap is anchored to the shinbone with a ligament. When the quadriceps contract, the kneecap slides up the groove in the femur, as shown in the lower drawing, pulling the lower leg straight at the same time.*

tibia—the shinbone, or main bone of the lower leg. The weight of the body thus holds the joint together, pressing the balls of the thighbone into the sockets of the shinbone. The hamstrings extend over the joint at the rear, and when they are contracted, they flex the knee.

Considering the powerful forces involved, the problem of straightening the knee out again is more difficult, because the attachment of the quadriceps muscles has to extend across the protruding part of the joint. The kneecap is evolution's solution to the problem. Instead of having a tendon extend over the joint, with the resulting problems of strain, friction, and possible slippage, the tendons of the quadriceps attach to a free piece of bone, the kneecap. This is positioned on the front of the joint and is attached to the lower leg by a group of ligaments. Thus if you extend your leg and relax the muscles, you will find that the kneecap is quite loose and can be moved around with the fingers. When the muscles at the front of the thigh are tensed, the kneecap is pulled tight.

Because of its function as a link between the lower leg and the quadriceps muscle, the kneecap rides up and down somewhat during normal movement of the leg. It is kept in position because it rides in the groove between the two balls at the bottom of the fibula, as shown in the illustration. A raised portion at the back of the kneecap rides up and down in this groove. But any rough areas, damage to the kneecap, or misalignment of either the thighbone or the lower leg can pull the kneecap out of line, and this is when *runner's knee* or *chondromalacia of the patella* occurs. One factor that can throw the lower leg out of alignment is excessive movement of the foot—a subject to which we now should turn.

CHAPTER 18

Structural Problems of the Feet

T HE EFFECTS that the feet can have on the legs and even on the hips and lower back have been mentioned throughout this book. To understand how these injuries occur, however, it is necessary to look at how the feet move during running. The structure of the foot is nearly as complex as that of the hand, which it closely resembles. The foot does not have quite so much freedom of motion, but it has to withstand far more stress, particularly if it happens to belong to a runner.

The feet serve several functions during running. They bear all the body weight, of course, and transmit the very considerable forces of acceleration and deceleration between the body and the ground. They also have a fairly wide range of

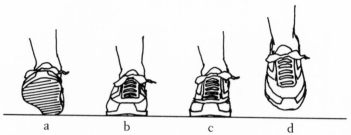

a	b	c	d

Pronation and supination, shown during running. In a the runner's foot is just starting to hit the ground and is about to begin pronation, rolling down and inward. In b the foot has completely pronated. Note that it is relaxed and tilting inward. It will now begin supination, so that it can become a rigid lever for takeoff. In c the foot has begun supination and the joints have locked. Note that the foot has shifted outward, no longer tilting in. In d supination continues as the foot leaves the ground, beginning to move toward the position it had when the heel first touched the ground.

motion around the axis of the leg, so that they can serve to maintain balance and can adapt to uneven ground. Finally, the foot acts to cushion the landing on the ground and then converts itself into a rigid lever to push back off. These last motions are rather complex, and they are made more so by the fact that the foot is at right angles to the rest of the body.

Pronation and Supination

The motions of the foot that are most difficult to understand are those of pronation and supination, because they are intricate and involve several joints simultaneously. The foot pronates as it comes into contact with the ground and takes on the weight of the body from the leg above. The normal motion of the foot during pronation is for the outside of the heel to hit first. The foot then rolls downward and inward, the ball of the foot comes into contact with the ground, and the joints of the foot relax as the foot spreads on the ground. This process of landing and weight shift is shown in the first two drawings.

At the same time that the foot is rolling inward, letting the weight of the body down slowly, the leg is moving forward on the ankle joint, effectively closing the angle between itself and the toes. What is not at all apparent unless you look carefully is that the leg is also rotating *inward*. Remember that in the last chapter it was pointed out that the leg rotates back and forth during running to accommodate to the turning pelvis, and that this rotation is transferred down as far as the foot. The rotation is accommodated by the action of pronation.

A little before the weight of the body moves directly over the foot, this whole rolling and rotational process reverses itself. The foot starts to roll up and outward. When this occurs, the joints below the anklebone in the back part of the foot lock where they had previously been flexible, and the foot becomes a rigid lever so that it can be used to drive off from the ground. The leg begins to rotate outward, and the foot is pushed downward away from the leg. This reversal is called supination, and it continues as the foot leaves the ground and is flexed with the inside higher, ready to hit the ground once again with the outside of the foot. Supination is shown in the second two drawings.

No attempt will be made here to describe the motions of each joint in the foot during pronation and supination. In fact, they vary somewhat with the individual stride. But the basic motion is important to an understanding of the overuse injuries caused by the foot because many of them are due to excessive or inadequate pronation.

The "Normal" Foot

When podiatrists refer to a "normal" foot, they mean something quite different from what most people understand from that word. The podiatrist means *normal* in the sense of *normative*, an ideal foot rather than an average one. The average foot is likely to be quite abnormal in this sense. The normal foot is one that transmits the forces from the leg to the ground and back without exerting any abnormal stresses on the leg or within the foot.

There are many characteristics that podiatrists believe a normal foot should have. It should be able to flex up toward the leg a moderate amount, for example. Otherwise you won't be able to walk or run forward normally without coming up almost immediately onto the ball of your foot, well before the normal propulsive phase. Most of the important characteristics can be observed by looking at the foot in mid-stance, as the weight of the body is moving directly over the weight-bearing foot. By this time, the shock of landing and adaptation to terrain should be over, and the foot should be transforming itself into a rigid lever in preparation for pushing off. Pronation therefore should have stopped, and the foot should already have begun supination.

During pronation the heel normally tilts over slightly inward, but it straightens up with supination. At mid-stance the heel should be straight, the lower leg should be straight over it, and the weight of the body should be supported directly down through these bones, without the toes or the sides of the feet having to claw, grip, or push in a strained way to maintain balance. The heel bone may be tilted in either direction during mid-stance in an abnormal foot, and this will put stress on the joint and on the bones. It may require the tendons and muscles to strain for stability. It may also transmit the strain up through the leg bones to the knee.

At mid-stride the bones leading out to the forefoot should also be stable. The far ends of the bones leading out to the toes, which form the bony structure of the ball of the foot, should all rest flat on the ground. These five bones running along the top of the foot are the *metatarsal bones*, and their knobby ends are the *metatarsal heads*. If some of these heads do not rest firmly on the ground at mid-stance, it will be hard to balance, and stresses will again be placed on the feet and legs. The toes themselves should rest on the surface of the ground, and not be curled or clawing.

Finally, the toes and the arch should provide firm support. If the big toe is floppy, so that the metatarsal head easily moves upward, the foot will tend to collapse inward, pronating excessively. A weak big toe with too much motion is called Morton's Toe, and it is often significantly shorter than the second toe.

Similarly, if the arch collapses inward and remains collapsed at midstance, the whole foot is remaining pronated when it shouldn't. This will make it difficult to push off correctly, because the foot cannot become a rigid lever. A strain on both the foot and the Achilles will result. The pronation at mid-stance is also likely to transmit rotational strain up into the knee, causing difficulties there.

The normal foot, then, is one that is structurally the soundest, operating in the correct mode to serve the runner most efficiently. There are many obvious abnormalities that will not be mentioned here. If overuse injuries begin to plague a runner with unusual feet, a visit to a sports podiatrist is an obvious step. What will be discussed here are the more subtle variations that can cause problems, the ones that are abnormal in the sense that they are less than ideal rather than noticeably peculiar. Some of these abnormalities can be fairly easily recognized by the runner, and the knowledge can be useful. Self-treatment is sometimes a perfectly reasonable procedure. Many people who suffer from mild overpronation, for example, can run quite comfortably with mass-produced or homemade supports.

The recognition of a foot abnormality is also worthwhile, because if during well-designed training you begin to suffer symptoms of a sort frequently caused by your foot type, you will know that it is time to see the podiatrist.

On the other hand, many of the imbalances of the feet are subtle, and recognizable only through careful and trained observation and measurement. It would be difficult or impossible for even an expert podiatrist to measure his own feet and legs. You can't analyze or even observe the way your heels move with any reasonable method. You can't measure leg length or many other parameters. Nor can you expect to understand the more complicated foot abnormalities. A heel that tilts outward and a forefoot inclined inward, for example, will be hard for you to diagnose and absurd to try to correct. Leave it to the experts. Any symptoms of overuse in the feet or knees that cannot be attributed to overtraining or to an easily understood problem with the feet or shoes should send you to the nearest good podiatrist.

Abnormal Feet

The most common structural weaknesses of the feet are those that result in excessive pronation and pronation that is not reversed to supination when it should be. Many cases of so-called flatfeet are due to excessive pronation. The arch of the foot is quite apparent when no load is placed on the foot, but it disappears under the weight of the body, because the foot has rolled over to conceal it. Excessive pronation can result from several causes. When the foot is in a relaxed position, the inside edge of the forefoot may be higher than the outside edge, so that the whole foot tilts over to compensate when it is bearing weight. Or the entire foot may be tilted this way, with a similar result. Bowlegs can also cause excessive pronation, as can a short, weak first toe.

Overpronation can contribute to a very large range of injuries, even including back pain if the overpronation occurs in only one foot, thereby effectively shortening that limb when it is being used. Most common, however, are strains in the arch and plantar fascia, knee problems, shinsplints, and a vulnerability to Achilles tendonitis. Overpronation can also contribute to various stress fractures. This sort of foot is often referred to as *unstable*, because it does not become adequately rigid during the later phase of the stride. Besides flatfeet, some of the signs of unstable feet are shoes that wear badly on the outside edge of the heel and the far inside edge of the toe, difficulty in balancing on one bare foot, particularly if the foot tends to roll inward, and heels that cant inward during the stride. Some of the ways of supporting unstable feet are discussed below.

Feet that are excessively rigid and allow too little pronation are somewhat less common, and they are also more difficult to deal with. Feet with very high, rigid arches might be included in this category, along with those that naturally cant outward, so that the shoes wear along the entire outside edge of the sole. Rigid feet like these often absorb very little of the force impact during foot strike, transmitting it up the leg instead. Stresses are felt through the entire leg, excessive strain is put on the plantar fascia, and the big toe may have to press down to meet the ground. This sort of "rigid foot" may also be associated with tight calf muscles or joint deformities that don't permit the foot to bend up from the horizontal.

Aside from obvious deformities that are apparent to anyone, the heel or the forefoot can be angled naturally during the weight-bearing part of the stride in either direction from the neutral position. This will cause stresses in the foot and the leg during running unless some kind of support can be provided. Thus, if the forefoot is naturally raised on the inside, so that the foot has to twist for the big toe to reach the ground (forefoot varus), the foot will be forced to pronate excessively as the runner puts weight on it. A forefoot that tilts outward is thus one of the causes of excessive pronation. If the heel tilts the same way, the effect will be even more pronounced. If the inside of the foot is supported, however, effectively bringing the ground up to meet the foot partway, the excessive pronation will be reduced or will not occur, and any overuse symptoms associated with it may disappear. This type of support, essentially changing the surface that the foot meets, is the main basis for the type of orthotic supports made by podiatrists. It is also the technique used for most self-treatment.

Analyzing Your Gait

As mentioned before, there are a whole series of variations in the angulation of the heel and the forefoot, and combinations of the two. Measuring these is difficult and takes a skillful practitioner, but the runner does not really have to throw up his hands completely in considering foot problems. If you think about your running and are aware of the way your feet land, you can deduce most of the characteristics of your gait. The way your shoes wear can tell you a great deal, particularly if you examine a pair of running shoes that have not been regularly glued. You can also learn a lot from looking at your footprints when you run in snow, mud, or wet sand. If the footprints of one foot angle out ten degrees more than the other, you don't need a doctor to tell you that one of the joints in that leg is different from the other. If your shoes are worn completely along the insides and very little on the outsides, it is easy to tell that your feet are angled so that the insides are lower, though you may not be able to deduce the fine points, such as which joint in the ankle is causing the pattern. Calluses on the feet are even more significant and will be considered in a moment.

The pattern of the foot landing is one of the first things to examine when you are trying to understand your own gait and foot structure. After you have run through a puddle or some snow, go back and look at the line of footprints. A normal gait will result in a line of tracks with the inside edges of the feet running pretty much in a straight line along the course you are following. Since the forefoot is wider than the heel, the tracks will appear to toe out very slightly. (During walking the toe-out is more marked; during running the feet hit a little straighter.) If one or both of your feet toe in or out significantly, it is almost certainly due to a discrepancy in the leg. The pattern of the shoe wear and perhaps stress on the feet will also be predictable. Wear along the outer edge of the shoe would be expected if your foot toes in, for example. If one foot toes out, you would expect wear to be accentuated on the outside of the heel and the inside of the toe on that shoe.

The wear on the shoe for a normal foot follows the pattern you would expect from the landing sequence of the pronating foot. Since you land first on the outside of your heel, wear normally occurs to the outside of the center of the heel. Wear on the *far* outside edge is indicative of a deformity, though not necessarily one that will cause injury. Most wear on sole material occurs during the twisting and scuffing of takeoff and landing, so the additional area of wear on a normal shoe is around the ball of the foot, concentrating somewhat toward the inside, in the area where the first metatarsal head pushes off. There is also some wear that extends on out to the toes, especially around the big toe. Thus a shoe with a wear pattern concentrating along the outside edge of the sole tells you the foot is not really pronating and taking off normally. If your shoe wears out this way, and you develop symptoms typical of a rigid foot pattern, it would be wise to consult with a podiatrist.

A shoe wear pattern with most of the tread ground off on the outside of the heel and far to the inside of the front of the shoe indicates that the heel strikes fairly normally, but that the foot then slops over and does not supinate fully during takeoff. Symptoms characteristic of excessive pronation would show a need for support along the inside of the foot. Shoes with heavy wear all along the insides show excessive pronation throughout the gait; again, if symptoms associated with excessive pronation occur, it is a good indication that you need support on the inside edges of your feet.

Calluses on the feet may also give clues about abnormal stresses. Unlike shoe wear patterns, which show variations from the norm but do not necessarily indicate that your feet are being subjected to excessive stress, calluses are a sure sign that such stress exists. They are additional layers of skin produced to protect the foot. Thus, if you walk barefoot a lot, your feet will become callused to protect the soles against injury from abrasion and cuts.

Calluses and corns on particular areas of the foot build up because of unusual pressure or shearing stresses. They may result from shoes that are badly chosen or that fit poorly. Otherwise they indicate a structural problem in the foot. This is especially true of the deep type of callus or corn that is caused by the shearing force of the tissue being moved over the bone. For example, calluses often build up under one or two metatarsal heads that are taking an abnormal share of stress.

Analysis of the structure of the feet and legs, together with careful diagnosis of injuries, will often enable the trainer, podiatrist, or orthopedist to come up with plans of treatment that will allow the runner with structural problems to run pain free. If a problem has become acute, especially if it has been allowed to go on for a long time, a whole series of treatments may be necessary to help heal the damage already done. Most problems caused by minor structural defects, however, can be treated successfully with a program of appropriately graded rest and training combined with stretching exercises and support for the feet.

Foot Support

Feet with structural problems cannot usually be changed for the better in mature people. The purpose of foot supports is to change the way the forces act between the ground and the feet so that you can run comfortably and without injury. In many cases proper support for the feet can make amazing differences in the runner's capacity to train without injury. Supports are not a panacea, however, and they will not always compensate completely for basic foot defects. They will almost certainly be a disappointment if you do not follow the other rules for dealing with injury. Podiatrists have sometimes been too quick to assume that a set of orthotics would solve all of a runner's difficulties. This is why it is important to use your own common sense, whether you are treating an injury yourself or seeing a specialist.

The function of a foot support is to bring the ground up to meet the foot at selected places so that the foot does not have to twist abnormally to bear weight. But because the force of gravity still pulls straight down, and because the foot must be permitted to flex and shoes permitted to cushion impact, the degree to which the foot can be practically supported is limited. The best control short of building custom shoes is achieved with a molded plastic form for the bottom of the foot, which cups under the heel of the foot and extends to just behind the metatarsal heads. Such supports are cast to the shape of the bottom of the foot in a neutral position and are fairly stiff, so they are usually called *rigid orthotics*, though they do have some ability to flex. The physician can then place cants or shims on the bottom of the orthotic to adjust the angulation of the foot to correct structural difficulties. Not all foot problems require rigid orthotics, however. Rigid orthotics provide maximum control, but they create some problems of their own, and many podiatrists prefer to try soft supports first.

It is worth recalling here that one of the primary indications that an injury is being caused by structural defects in your legs or feet is that it appears when you reach a certain level of training, no matter how slowly you work up to it. When such symptoms occur, don't allow them to persist for long periods. If they are serious, see a specialist right away. If they are mild, you may want to seek medical help or to try solving the problem yourself.

Some of the newer shoe designs with built-in support are

worth trying to see if they will control excessive foot motion enough to allow injuries to heal. Many more will undoubtedly appear on the market, but good examples are the Etonic Street Fighter and the Brooks Vantage Supreme. These shoes provide good cushioning as well as good support, and cushioning is an important factor when you are fighting an injury. The Etonic has a stiff foam insert designed to provide some support against excessive pronation, while the Brooks has an insole that is built up along the inside edge to produce a similar effect.

It is important to note that no support will work unless the shoe is built in such a way as to provide a suitable foundation. An orthotic or an arch support inserted in the shoe will have no effect if the sole does not extend far enough under the arch to hold the support. Control of the motion of the heel cannot be achieved unless the heel of the shoe itself is wide enough in proportion to its height to hold the supporting system firmly. The shoe and the support must also be matched. I have seen orthotics with heel-control posts that were positioned exactly over a hollow in the heel of the shoe they were made to fit, so that instead of holding the inside of the heel up, they pushed the insole down into the hollow. As a result, the posted orthotic was giving no control of the heel at all—though it was making a mess of the shoe.

Another way to provide support is to purchase a ready-made support. There are a number of types available, and more are appearing now that the demand is becoming clear. Most medical supply houses specializing in orthopedic and surgical appliances carry standard leather arch supports, which work fairly well. Several supports made by Dr. Scholl have been used successfully in the past, but their new Runner's Wedge support seems likely to be the best for runners to try. It provides some extra cushioning and heel control, together with some elevation of the inside of the heel to help prevent excessive pronation at the time the heel first strikes the ground.

The new shoes and ready-made supports are beginning to make some of the older makeshift alternatives obsolete, but some runners may still find it helpful to provide more positive arch support. The best of the newer shoes do give reasonable arch control, but the conventional soft sponge insert under the arch gives virtually no support under the impact of running. Firmer rubber inserts of the same shape, called arch cookies, can be obtained in three different sizes from New Balance Shoe Company, 38 Everett Street, Boston, Massachusetts 02134. These arch cookies can be glued in any shoe to replace the soft sponge rubber support that is in the shoe when you buy it. You will have to experiment to see whether it is best to place the arch cookie above or below the insole. Once you have found the best position, use contact cement to fasten the arch cookie in the shoe.

Sponge rubber inserts should be removed before adding any special support to a shoe, whether it is an orthotic made by a specialist or a mass-produced support. The extra elevation of the sponge insert will make the insert fit incorrectly. Two other problems are commonly associated with inserts of all kinds: excessive heel elevation and blistering under the supported areas of the foot.

Shoes that have low heel counters cannot always be used with supports that raise the heel even slightly, including both custom-made and over-the-counter varieties. If the upper edge of the shoe heel digs into the Achilles tendon when your heel is raised by the support, you are likely to have trouble with tendonitis or bursitis of the heel. Make sure that the heel of the shoe still fits comfortably with the insert, and be alert during the first few weeks of running with a support for problems caused by the change in fit.

All supports can cause blistering when you begin to wear them, because if they support areas of the foot that did not bear weight before, there will be friction and pressure on untoughened skin. The problem will be worse if the surface of the support is badly designed for the purpose. Arch cookies, including those that come in shoes, are terrible in this respect. Runners who actually need support at the arch will find that the rubber surface raises horrible blisters, whether or not socks are worn. Rigid orthotics with no covering material are almost as bad. Orthotics can be padded with a nylon-backed neoprene foam (one-eighth inch thick) glued to the top of the orthotic with contact cement. The foam should extend an inch or so past the front of the orthotic to cover the area under the ball of the foot. Such neoprene-nylon material is marketed for the purpose by the Spenco Company. It is also used for making wet suits, so it can also be purchased more cheaply from shops catering to divers, surfers, and kayakers. Arch cookies can be made smooth by cutting a piece of lightweight nylon fabric to fit over the top and gluing it on with contact cement.

Taping and Using Foam Supports

If you suspect that your feet need support, one of the best ways to find out whether it will help is by making supports from a sheet of adhesive-backed foam and taping them on your feet. The tape will serve to keep the temporary foam supports from peeling off or slipping and will also provide a good deal of support itself for those who pronate excessively. The materials used can be obtained from a medical supply house selling orthopedic devices. You need plain adhesive tape (not the plastic kind) 1½ inches and 2 inches wide, adhesive-backed felt ¼-inch thick, and adhesive-backed foam ¼-inch thick. If you pronate excessively at the heel, first make a heel wedge to go in the heel of your shoe to support the inside of your heel, using the felt material, which does not compress as much as the foam. It should be full thickness at the inside of the heel (big toe side) and should extend 2 inches from the side and 3 inches forward. Taper the felt with a razor blade on the nonadhesive side so that it angles evenly down from full height at the inside edge of the shoe to a wedge point where it stops, two thirds of the way across the shoe. Taper the wedge at the front just enough to make the foot comfortable. Adjust the wedge until it is comfortable, and then take off the backing and glue it into the shoe.

Padding for the arch, and the forefoot if it is needed there, is made from the foam material, which is easy to shape with scissors. A large arch cookie with tapered edges under the arch helps most runners who suffer from excessive pronation. If you have signs of extreme pronation at the front of the foot, extend this pad under the first metatarsal head (the ball of the foot behind the big toe). This would be called for if you have a short, very flexible big toe, if you develop calluses and corns under the second metatarsal, or if your shoe wears out far to the inside of the foot. Otherwise, taper the arch pad off behind the ball of the foot. Stick the foam pad in place, and then tape the foot as shown in the illustrations of the low Dye strapping, a method that does not require shaving the foot and that gives a good deal of support. This strapping is also used as a base for taping a sprained ankle with the high-Dye strapping.

If either the heel wedge or the tape and foam support helps

Low Dye strapping for the foot. This strapping can be used to help support the foot against excessive pronation or to support the arch, usually with arch pads included in the taping. It can also be used as a base for the high Dye strapping that follows. No shaving of the foot is necessary for the low Dye strapping.

a–c   *Tape around from the outside to the inside of the foot as shown, with three pieces of 1½-inch tape. Start each on the outside of the foot below the protrusion of the fibula, overlapping as shown. The tape should be firm, but avoid pulling it tight, which will cause wrinkles and discomfort. The foot should be tilted slightly outward (supinated) throughout the taping.*

d–g   *Place four pieces of 2-inch tape five inches long as stirrups under the foot as shown. Begin sticking each piece at the center of the foot, and stick toward both ends at the same time. Again the tape should be firm, but not pulled tight.*

h   *Cover the ends of the stirrups with a piece of 2-inch tape, as shown.*

i   *Place a 3-inch length of 2-inch tape sticky side up on top of the metatarsals, as shown. This protects the hair on top of the foot.*

j   *Run a piece of 2-inch tape all the way around the foot as shown to anchor the strapping just behind the ball of the foot.*

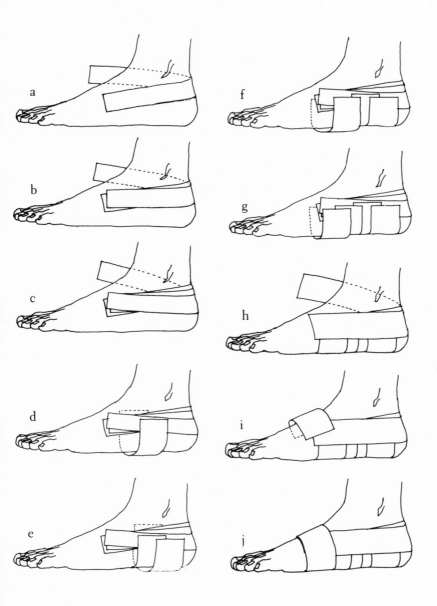

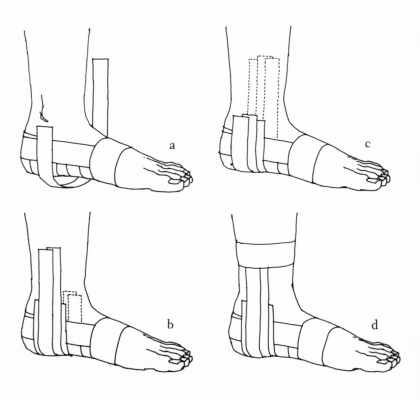

High Dye strapping for a sprain (the ankle area must be shaved).
Begin by applying a low Dye strapping as shown in illustration
#2.

a Apply a 1½-inch piece of tape 13 inches long, beginning just in
   front of and below the inside ankle bone, extending under the heel
   and up the other side of the ankle.

b Apply two more 13-inch pieces of tape overlapping the first one,
   each one ½ inch to the rear.

c Apply two 13-inch pieces of tape as shown beginning under the
   outside ankle bone, and extending under the heel toward the inside.

d Anchor the tape of the straps with a piece of 2-inch tape around
   the upper ankle.

alleviate your symptoms, it is a good indication that you need more permanent supports in your shoes. See a specialist, or try some of the over-the-counter supports or special shoes. Remember that reduced training, religiously performed stretching, and foot exercises are essential to healing along with support of the foot. If self-help methods improve your condition but don't completely solve the problem, see a podiatrist or an orthopedist. Remember that the goal of running should be enjoyment and fitness, not a test of your pain threshold.

Additional Reading

THE RUNNER looking for help with his injuries is likely to become rather frustrated in poring through the literature on the subject. The best sources are in specialized medical journals, but these are likely to be difficult because of technical terminology as well as hard to locate. The best ones on mechanical problems written from a podiatric point of view are *Podiatric Sports Medicine* by Steven Subotnick (Mount Kisco, New York: Futura, 1975) and *The Foot Book* by Harry Hlavac (Mountain View, California: World Pubns., 1977). Both will require some application from the lay reader; Subotnick is a little more detailed but presumes more background. Also useful is the American Academy of Orthopedic

Surgeons' *Symposium on Sports Medicine* (St. Louis: Mosby, 1969).

George Sheehan's *Encyclopedia of Athletic Medicine* (Mountain View, California: World, 1972) is written for runners and has some excellent articles. Dr. Sheehan's regular column of medical advice in *Runner's World* magazine (monthly, P.O. Box 366, Mountain View, California 94042) is always entertaining and often enlightening. Some of his past advice is compiled in *Medical Advice for Runners* (New York: Simon & Schuster, 1978). Dr. Gabe Mirkin, another physician with a long-term interest in running, writes a medical column for a newer magazine, *The Runner* (monthly, P.O. Box 2730, Boulder, Colorado 80321).

The best book on yoga stretching is B.K.S. Iyengar's *Light on Yoga* (New York: Schocken, 1966). An excellent book on stretching techniques for those not interested in the yoga discipline is Bob Anderson's *Stretching*, available from the author at P.O. Box 2734, Fullerton, California 92633. Anderson includes some exercises as well. The best book on resistance exercises for runners is John Jesse's *Strength, Power and Muscular Endurance for Runners and Hurdlers* (Pasadena, California: Athletic Press, 1971).

INDEX

Accidental injuries, 157–169

Achilles tendon, 213; injury to, 58, 61, 63, 85, 102; and shoes, 70, 74; stretch for, 127

Ankles, 211; exercises for, 139–141; injury to, 43, 104, 175–177

Arthritis, 56

Athlete's foot, 39–40

Back, injury to, 41–42, 49–50, 78–80; stretches for, 131, 133, 136

Beginner, and running, 7–11

Blisters, 29–36

Bone injury, 58–60

Bursitis, 60, 62, 88–91, 103, 188–189

Calf, 97–101, 127, 213

Calisthenics, 119–120, 153

Calluses, 36–37, 225–226

Cartilage, 56–57

Chafing, 28–29

Chondromalacia of the patella, 62, 95–97, 215

Clothing, 182–184, 196–197

Colds, and running, 178–179

Conditioning, 9–11, 142–154

Corns, 36–37, 226

Cramps, 40–41, 200

Dehydration, 197–198, 200

Drinking, 197–198

Dye strapping, 231–235

Exercises, 26–27, 138–141; *see also* Stretching

Eyes, protecting, 168

Feet, abnormal, 221–223; exercises for, 139–141; injury to, 49–50, 61, 62–63, 104–106; "normal," 219–221; structural problems with, 49–50, 216–235

Flatfeet, 221

Fractures, 58–59

Frostbite, 185–187

Gait, analyzing, 223–226

Groin, 91, 135, 213

Hamstrings, 128, 129, 131, 135, 212–213

Hazards to runners, 158–169

Heart, 7–8

Heat injuries, 190–200

Heels, 61, 63, 101–104

Hips, 86–91, 129–130, 211

Hypothermia, 179–184

Ice, 80–81, 168–169

Injuries, 43–63, 77–107

Joints, 56–57, 210

Knees, 62, 91–97, 213–215

Ligaments, 56, 210

Marathons, 14, 16, 67–68

Medical help, 108–113

Morton's toe, 220

Muscles, 48, 82–84, 211

Numbness, 42

Overtraining, 12–15, 20–22, 46–50, 53–54

Palpation, 84–85

Podiatrist, 112–113

Pronation, 217–218, 221, 225

Quadriceps, 213

Racing, 67–68

Running surface, 51

Sciatica, 79–80, 87–88

Shinsplints, 59, 97–101, 213

Shoes, 47, 48, 69–76, 224–235

Shoulders, 41–42, 137

Skin, 28–37

Spine, 49–50, 88

Sprains, 51, 55, 171–176

Spurs, 61, 62

Stitches, 40–41

Stomach pain, 40

Strain, 54–55, 172–173

Stress, 7–9, 13–15, 59, 101

Stretching, 26–27, 48, 49, 117–123, 125–137

Sunburn, 200

Supination, 217–218

Support, foot, 226–235

Taping, 175–177, 230–235

Tendon strain, 51, 54–55, 57–58, 60, 85–86

Thighs, 91, 211

Tightness, 48, 126

Toenails, 37–39

Training, 17–20, 65–69

Warts, 37

Weather, 44

Weight, 24–25, 153

Yoga, 121, 125, 126, 133